WALKING WITH GOD

WALKING WITH GOD

J.C. RYLE

Foreword by Derek Prime

An easier to read and abridged version of
Practical Religion
by Bishop J.C. Ryle

Prepared by
Gilbert McAdam,
Pastor of Trinity Baptist Church,
Broughty Ferry,
Dundee

Joint Managing Editors
J.P. Arthur M.A.
H.J. Appleby

© GRACE PUBLICATIONS TRUST
139 Grosvenor Avenue
London, N5 2NH,
England

First published 1995

ISBN 0 946462 37 2

Distributed by:
EVANGELICAL PRESS
12 Wooler Street
Darlington
Co. Durham DL1 1RQ
England

Printed in Great Britain by
Cox & Wyman Ltd, Reading.

Cover design: L.L. Evans

CONTENTS

Page

About the Author   6

Foreword   7

1.   Self-Examination   9
2.   Effort   17
3.   Reality   25
4.   Prayer   30
5.   Bible Reading   41
6.   Love   52
7.   Zeal   56
8.   Happiness   61
9.   Formality   67
10. The World   73
11. Wealth and Poverty   81
12. The Best Friend   88
13. Illness   94
14. The Family of God   103
15. Heirs of God   108
16. The Great Gathering   117
17. The Great Separation   121
18. Eternity   128

Appendix: The Lord's Day   136

About the Author

John Charles Ryle (1816-1900) was the son of a wealthy banker and was educated at Eton and Christ Church College, Oxford. He was a good athlete, and rowed and played cricket for Oxford University. He obtained a first class honours degree, but turned down the offer of a college fellowship. Instead, he began a career in law, intending to enter the House of Commons. However, he experienced evangelical conversion in 1838, through hearing the second chapter of Ephesians read in church, and in 1841 he entered the ministry of the Church of England.

After serving in four parish churches, in Hampshire and Suffolk, he was appointed in 1880 as the first Bishop of the new diocese of Liverpool. Throughout his ministry he contended fearlessly for the great truths of the Word of God. His literary output was immense, and his tracts reached a circulation of over twenty million. His books include *The True Christian*, *The Upper Room*, *Old Paths*, *Holiness* and *Practical Religion*, and *Expository Thoughts* on each of the four Gospels. C.H. Spurgeon considered him "the best man in the Church of England", and in a memorial sermon preached on the Sunday after Bishop Ryle's funeral, his friend Richard Hobson said, "I am bold to say that perhaps few men in the nineteenth century did so much for God, for truth, for righteousness, among the English-speaking race and in the world as our late Bishop."

Note

Walking with God has been simplified and abridged from the 1959 edition of *Practical Religion* published by James Clarke and Co. Ltd., Cambridge. That edition omitted two chapters from the original, and the present abridgment has omitted one further chapter, on "The Lord's Supper". The Appendix on "The Lord's Day" has been simplified and abridged from another book of Bishop Ryle's, *Knots Untied*, where it appears under the title of "The Sabbath".

FOREWORD

The first book I read by J.C. Ryle was *Holiness*, and it had a profound effect upon me for good. The second was *Practical Religion*. I do not know how it came into my possession. It was clearly a book that I acquired as a gift as a fairly young minister. I immediately discovered its value, for I made my personal index of its contents, and have turned to it many times over the years.

Few nineteenth century writers retain the freshness and relevance of J.C. Ryle. *Practical Religion* lives up to its title. Each chapter is easy reading, well structured, and goes to the heart of the matters under discussion.

Ryle is worthy of reading on a number of scores. First, he is always biblical, not simply because he quotes Scripture, but because he has so well imbibed its teaching that all he says flows from it. Second, he relates everything to the saving work of our Lord Jesus Christ, never allowing the reader to forget that the proper response to grace is gratitude and change of lifestyle. Third, he is eminently practical. He enunciates principles, and demonstrates their application in daily life. Fourth, he deals with subjects which are often neglected, but are of perpetual relevance to the Christian, such as the sections on self-examination and the Christian's attitude to the world.

I am glad that the chapter on "The Lord's Day" has been added, since it is a model of simplicity, the clear statement of biblical principles, and their application in an eminently reasonable and down-to-earth manner.

The abridgement loses nothing of the urgent practical and pastoral spirit that characterises Ryle. Both Christians and those seeking the truth about God and his Son Jesus Christ will find instruction, challenge and encouragement.

Derek Prime
Edinburgh

1.
SELF-EXAMINATION

"Let us now go back and visit our brethren in every city where we have preached the word of the Lord, and see how they are doing." - Acts 15:36

After their first missionary journey together, the Apostle Paul suggested to Barnabas that they should re-visit the churches they had founded to see how they were getting on. He was anxious to know whether they were growing as Christians. So he said, "Let us go back and visit our brethren and see how they are doing." There is something we can learn from this we need to examine ourselves to see how *we* are getting on in our relationship with God.

We live in an age of great *spiritual privileges*. The gospel has been preached almost throughout the whole world. The Bible is available in more languages than ever before. In many parts of the world the church has grown with great speed. But we must ask ourselves, "Are *we* any better because of it?"

We live in an age of great *spiritual danger*. Never before have so many people throughout the world professed to be Christians. But are they all converted? Many like to attend large meetings, where exciting things are happening. But looking for excitement is a different thing from *growing* as a Christian, and it is of great importance that we sometimes stop and ask ourselves where we really are spiritually.

Let me suggest to you ten questions to help you discover the truth about your spiritual condition. I ask these questions only for your good. If at first some of them seem to be rather harsh, remember that the person who tells you the most truth is in reality your best friend.

1. Do you ever think about your spiritual condition at all?

Sadly, there are many who never think at all about salvation. They never stop to think seriously about death and judgment, about eternity, about heaven and hell. They are too concerned with business, pleasure, their family, politics or money. They live as though they were never going to die and stand before the judgment of God. Such people are really bringing themselves down to the level of the animals, for they never think about the most important matters of life. Do *you* think about these things?

2. Do you ever do anything about your salvation?

There are many who sometimes think about Christianity, but who never get any further than thinking. Perhaps when they are in trouble, or someone has just died, or perhaps when they have met a real Christian or read a Christian book they think a good deal about it. But that is where they stop. They do not separate themselves from serving sin and the sinful world; they do not take up their cross and follow Christ. Remember - it is not enough just to think about God and about salvation. You must *do* something about it or you cannot be saved.

3. Are you trying to satisfy your conscience with outward religion?

Many make this mistake. Their Christianity consists entirely in outward duties. They attend all the meetings for worship. They are never missing from the Lord's Supper. They may hold very strongly to the particular teachings of their church, and argue with anyone who does not agree with them. Yet for all this, there is no devotion to Christ in their *hearts*. Their religion does not satisfy them, for they know nothing of inward joy and peace. Perhaps secretly in their hearts they know that something is wrong, but they don't know what. I appeal to you, then, to examine yourself. If you care about your salvation, do not rest content with mere outward observances. You must have much more than that to be saved.

4. Have your sins been forgiven?

You know in your heart that you are a sinner - that you have fallen short of God's standards in thought, in word and in deed. You know, therefore, that if on the last day your sins have not been forgiven, you must be condemned for ever. Now it is the glory of the Christian faith that it provides exactly the forgiveness that you need - complete, free, eternal forgiveness. This forgiveness has been bought for us by the Lord Jesus Christ, by his coming into the world to be our Saviour, and by his living, dying and rising again as our substitute. But although this forgiveness is perfectly free, it is not given to us automatically. You do not receive it simply by going to a Christian church, or even by becoming a member of one. It is something which each person must take hold of for himself by exercising personal *faith*. If you do not make it your own by faith, then as far as you are concerned Christ might as well not have died. Faith is simply a humble, sincere trust in the Lord Jesus to save you. All who personally trust in him are immediately accepted and forgiven, but without this trust there is no forgiveness at all.

So you see it is not enough simply to know the facts about the Lord Jesus Christ. You know that he is the Saviour of men, but is he *your* Saviour? Do you know that *your* sins are forgiven?

5. Have you experienced the reality of conversion to God?

"Unless you are converted and become as little children, you will by no means enter the kingdom of heaven" (Matthew

11

18:3). "If anyone is in Christ he is a new creation" (2 Corinthians 5:17). By nature we are so weak, earthly-minded and sinful that without a complete change we cannot serve God in this life, and could not enjoy him in heaven. Just as ducks when they are born naturally take to water, so when we are born we naturally take to sin. If we are to leave sin and learn to love God, a great change must take place in our lives. And if that change has taken place, it will be seen by its fruits. Do you have a sense of sin and of hatred for it? Do you have faith in Christ and love for him? Do you love holiness, and long to be more holy? Do you find yourself growing in love for God's people and dislike of the ways of the world? These are the signs which always follow conversion to God. Where do *you* stand?

6. Do you know anything of practical Christian holiness?

The Bible makes it clear that "without holiness no one will see the Lord". Holiness is the invariable result of true conversion. Now holiness is not absolute perfection - absolute freedom from sin. That exists only in heaven. Neither is holiness something which we obtain without a constant fight and struggle. But although holiness in this life is imperfect, nevertheless it is real. Real holiness will make a man do his duty in his own home and at work and will affect the way he lives his daily life and copes with its problems. It will make him humble, kind, unselfish, considerate of others, loving and forgiving. It will not lead him away from the normal duties of daily life, but will enable him to live as a Christian wherever God has called him to be.

7. Do you know anything about enjoying the means of grace?

By "the means of grace" I mean five main things: reading the Bible, private prayer, meeting with other Christians for worship, taking the Lord's Supper and keeping the Lord's Day holy. These things God has graciously appointed either to bring us to faith in Christ or to help us make progress as Christians. Our spiritual condition will largely depend on the way in which we use them. Notice, I say the *way* we use them, for there is no automatic benefit in doing them. It is of great importance *how* we do them. So I must ask you, Do you find *delight* in reading God's Word? Do you *pour out your heart* to God in prayer? Is the Lord's Day a *delight* to you as you spend it in praise, prayer and Christian fellowship? Even if they had no other purpose, the "means of grace" would still be useful as pointers to our true spiritual condition. Tell me what a man does in relation to these things and I will soon tell you whether he is on the road to heaven or to hell.

8. Do you ever try to do any good in the world?

On earth, the Lord Jesus "went about doing good" (Acts 10:38). True Christians ever since have tried to follow his example. When the Lord Jesus told the story of the Good Samaritan (Luke 10:25-37) he ended by saying, "Go and do likewise." There are always opportunities for doing good. The only question is whether we really *want* to do it. Even those who have no money to give can do good to the sick and those with other problems, by being willing to spend time with them and by showing them sympathy and care. Read the story of the Good Samaritan. Do *you* know anything about this kind of love to others? Do you try to do good to others apart from your own friends, family and church? Are you living as a disciple of him who "went about doing good" and commanded us to follow him as our "example"? (John 13:15)

9. Do you know anything of living the life of habitual fellowship with Christ?

By "fellowship" I mean the habit of "abiding in Christ" which our Lord tells us is necessary if we are to bear fruit as Christians

(John 15:4-8). We must understand clearly that having fellowship with Christ is much more than simply being a Christian. All who have repented and come to Christ are Christians, and belong to him. But too many never get beyond this stage. Because of ignorance, laziness, fear of man, love of the world, or some besetting sin which has never been dealt with, they have only a little faith, a little hope, a little peace and a little holiness. They live all their lives bearing fruit only "thirtyfold" (Matthew 13:8).

Fellowship with Christ is different. It is something experienced by those who strive constantly to grow in grace: in faith, knowledge, conformity to Christ's will in everything. It is experienced by those who "press toward the goal" (Philippians 3:14). The great secret of fellowship is to be always living by faith in Christ, and continually drawing from him all the resources that we need. The Apostle Paul could say, "For to me, to live is Christ" (Philippians 1:21), and "It is no longer I who live, but Christ lives in me" (Galatians 2:20). This kind of fellowship is perfectly consistent with a deep conviction of our own sins and corruption. It does not deliver us from the experience described in the seventh chapter of Romans. But it does enable us to look away from ourselves to the Lord Jesus, and to rejoice in him.

10. Do you know anything of being ready for Christ's second coming?

It is one of the great certainties of the Bible that Christ will come to this world again. He will come both to punish sinners and to bring the salvation of his people to perfection in his everlasting kingdom of righteousness. Are you ready for his coming? To be ready involves nothing more than being a real, consistent Christian. It does not involve abandoning your daily work so as to be ready for him, but rather that you must do it as a Christian, with your heart always ready to leave everything when he appears. Again I ask you, Are you ready?

Conclusion

Let me finish with a few words of application.

1. Are you *asleep and thoughtless about spiritual realities?* Wake up! You are like someone sleeping in a boat drifting towards rocks which will destroy it. Wake up, and call upon God!

2. Are you *feeling self-condemned and afraid there is no hope for you?* Throw away your fears and listen to Christ. He says, "Come to me, all you who labour and are heavy laden, and I will give you rest" (Matthew 11:28). "The one who comes to me I will by no means cast out" (John 6:37). These words are for you as well as for others. Bring all your sin and guilt, your unbelief and doubt, your unfitness and weaknesses - bring them all to Christ. "This man receives sinners" (Luke 15:2). He will receive you. Call on him right now.

3. Do you *profess to be a believer in Christ, yet you have not much joy, peace and comfort?* Examine your heart today, and see whether the fault is not entirely your own. Probably you are making little or no effort, content with just a little faith, repentance and sanctification, and reluctant to be really zealous in the Christian life. If so, you will never be a happy Christian, unless you change your ways. Change today! Begin to be wholehearted in your Christianity. Strive to get nearer to Christ, to abide in him, to hold on to him, to sit at his feet like Mary, and to drink freely from the fountain of life. Only then will your joy be full.

4. Are you a believer, but *troubled with doubts and fears, because of your feebleness, weakness, and sense of sin?* Remember what the Bible says about Jesus: "A bruised reed he will not break, and smoking flax he will not quench" (Matthew 12:20). This text is for you. Even feeble faith is better than no faith. A small grain of life is better than no life. Perhaps you are expecting too much in this world, forgetting that you are not yet in heaven. You must expect little from yourself, but expect much from Christ. Look to Jesus more, and to yourself less.

5. Finally, are you *sometimes despondent* because of the trials you meet in life? Look up to Christ! He is altogether sympathetic, for he himself has suffered. He is at God's right hand. Pour out your heart to him. He can do more than feel sympathy with you: he can help you. You must learn to draw near to him. And remember - time is short. Soon it will be over and we shall be with the Lord. "For you have need of endurance, so that after you have done the will of God, you may receive the promise. For yet a little while and he who is coming will come, and will not tarry" (Hebrews 10:36,37).

2.
EFFORT

"Strive to enter through the narrow gate, for many, I say to you, will seek to enter and will not be able." - Luke 13:24

A man once asked the Lord Jesus Christ this question: "Lord, are there few who are saved?" The response of the Lord Jesus is very important. He said, "Strive to enter through the narrow gate." Whether few or many are saved does not affect *your* duty. Now is the time to be saved. You must strive to enter the gate *now*, for the day will come when many will seek to enter in but will not be able.

What the Lord Jesus says is very serious. His words remind us of our personal responsibility to be saved, and the immense danger of putting it off. May the Holy Spirit speak to the hearts of all who read, so that you may enter in and be saved! We shall consider the subject under three headings.

1. A description of the way of salvation

The Lord Jesus describes the way of salvation. He calls it "the narrow gate".

There is a gate which leads to forgiveness, peace with God and life in heaven. Everyone who enters through that gate will be saved. How much need we have of this gate! Sin is a great barrier between men and God. Man is a great sinner, and God is perfect in holiness. How can the two ever be brought together? Blessed be God, there is a way: a road, a gate, a path. This is the gate the Lord Jesus speaks about.

This gate was made for sinners by the Lord Jesus Christ. He planned it in eternity, and in time he came into the world and made this gate, by dying for sinners on the cross. He paid the debt of man's sin, and bore our punishment. This gate cost him his own body and blood. By his death he made a door by which sinners may enter the presence of God without fear. He made a road by which the greatest of sinners may draw near to God, if only they believe in him.

This gate is called the *narrow* gate, and with good reason. It is too narrow for those who love sin and are not willing to part with it. It is too narrow for those who love the sinful pleasures of the world, or who are not willing to take any trouble over the salvation of their souls. It is too narrow for those who are self-righteous and think they deserve to be saved because of their own goodness. For all such, the gate is too narrow to get through.

But it is the *only* gate through which you can get to heaven. There is no way round it, and no other gate. Everyone who is saved at all is saved *only* by Christ, and *only* by faith in him. You cannot merit salvation through repentance or good works. You must be saved through Christ alone!

But though this gate is narrow, it is a gate that is always ready to open. No sinner is ever forbidden to enter it: everyone who desires may enter it and be saved. The only condition is that you feel your sins and desire to be saved by Christ in his own way. Are you already conscious of your guilt and uncleanness? Then you may enter through this gate. It does not matter whether you are a great sinner, or whether you are elect or not. The only question is this: Do you feel your sins? Are you willing to put yourself into Christ's hands? If so, the gate will open to you at once. Enter it today!

Even though this gate is narrow, it is a gate through which thousands have entered and been saved. No sinner was ever turned away and told he was too bad. Some have been exceedingly bad, but they were not refused entry. As soon as they knocked, the One who built the gate gave orders that they should be let in.

18

King Manasseh, that evil king of Judah, came to this gate. He was guilty of idolatry and murder - even of his own children. But when his eyes were opened to see his sins, he ran to this gate and was let in.

Saul the Pharisee came to this gate. He had been a blasphemer of the Lord Jesus, and a persecutor of his people. He had tried to silence the gospel. But when he discovered his guilt and ran to this gate, it flew open for him and he was saved.

Many of the Jews who had crucified the Lord Jesus came to this gate. They had betrayed and crucified the Son of God. But in response to Peter's preaching, their hearts were pricked and the gate flew open and they were saved. And since the Bible was written, thousands upon thousands of people, from all countries and classes of society have come to this gate and been saved. My earnest desire is that you too should enter through it and be saved.

Consider what a great *privilege* it is to have such a gate at all. Many have lived and died without knowing of this gate, but you have it plainly set before you. You have Christ proclaimed to you. Salvation is set before you as a free gift. Be sure not to neglect this gate and perish because of unbelief.

And how *thankful* you should be if you have already entered through this gate! You are forgiven! You are ready for death and judgment, as well as for whatever may happen to you in this earthly life. What great reason you have to live a life of joy and praise for the mercy of God!

2. A plain command

Jesus commands us, "Strive to enter in." We can often learn much from a single word in the Bible, and we may certainly learn much from this one word "strive".

"STRIVE" teaches us that we must use diligently the means which God has appointed for us to seek him. We should attend diligently to reading the Bible and to hearing the Gospel preached.

19

"STRIVE" teaches us that God will deal with us as responsible beings. We must not sit down and do nothing, for Christ says to us, "Come - repent - believe - labour - ask - seek - knock." Our salvation is *entirely* of God, but our ruin if we are lost is *entirely* of ourselves.

"STRIVE" teaches us that we may expect opposition and a hard battle if our souls are to be saved. The devil will never let us escape without a struggle. Our own hearts which have loved sinful things will never be turned to spiritual things without difficulty. The world and its temptations will never be overcome without conflict. And none of this should surprise us, for neither in the natural nor in the spiritual realm is any great good done without great effort.

"STRIVE" teaches us that salvation is worth striving for. People strive for all kinds of things far less important than their salvation. Riches, greatness, education, promotion, are all corruptible. The incorruptible things are inside the narrow gate: the peace of God, the sense of the Holy Spirit dwelling in us, the knowledge that our sins are forgiven. These are things truly worth striving for!

"STRIVE" teaches us that it is sinful to be lazy in spiritual matters. God has commanded you to strive and you have no excuse if you refuse to do so.

"STRIVE" teaches us the great danger of being outside the narrow gate. To die outside the narrow gate is to be lost without hope for ever. The Lord Jesus saw that clearly. He knew the shortness and uncertainty of time, and he urges us not to delay, but to act quickly, not to leave it too late.

This word "strive" condemns many who call themselves Christians. They have been baptised and belong to the church. They do not murder or steal or commit adultery, but they certainly are not "striving" to be saved. They may be active enough in the things of this life, but in spiritual matters they make no efforts at all.

Many are irregular even in attending Sunday worship. That is not "striving". Many attend regularly but do so out of habit or because it is expected of them. That is not "striving". Many hardly ever read the Bible. They read newspapers, magazines and novels, but neglect the Word of God. That is not "striving". Many never pray. They get up without prayer and they go to bed without prayer. They ask nothing from God, and confess nothing to him. They do not thank him, nor seek him at all. They know they must die, yet they are not even on speaking terms with their Maker and their Judge! Is this "striving" to enter in? Let every man of common sense judge for himself.

I speak from my experience as a minister of the Gospel. It is painful to see how few "strive" to enter through the narrow gate. Many listen to God's Word preached. They do not argue against it. Yet neither do they "strive" to enter in and be saved. They will be earnest about the affairs of this life. They will strive to be rich and to succeed. That is not uncommon at all. But I see very few who "strive" to be saved.

Yet I am not surprised at all this. The parable of the great supper (Luke 14:16ff) is an exact picture of what I have seen myself since I became a minister - "men make excuses". One has his land to attend to, another his oxen to try out and another his family hindrances. But it grieves me deeply that men should have eternal life so close to them, and yet be lost because they will not "strive" to enter in.

I do not know the state of your heart, but I want to warn you against perishing for ever because you do not "strive". Do not suppose you must commit great crimes to be lost. The road of spiritual laziness - doing nothing - leads just as certainly to hell.

If you have already learned the need to "strive" for the good of your soul, I appeal to you never to think you are making too much effort - that you need not be so concerned. Beware of reducing your prayers, your Bible reading, your private times alone with God. Whatever you do, do it with all your heart and mind and strength. Never mind what anyone else thinks of you: your Master says, "STRIVE."

3. An awful prophecy

Jesus says, "Many will seek to enter and will not be able."

The Lord Jesus is speaking here of the time of his second coming to judge the world. He is speaking of the time when God's longsuffering will come to an end, when the throne of grace will be replaced by the throne of judgment, when the narrow gate will be barred and bolted, and the day of grace will be past for ever. The great Day of Judgment will come, and then these solemn words will be fulfilled: "Many will seek to enter and will not be able."

The time is coming when seeking God will be useless. Oh that men would remember that and seek him now! The Lord Jesus says that many shall be shut out of heaven for ever. He does not speak of ones and twos but of "many". Many will understand the truth too late - the truth of their own sinfulness and of God's holiness, the truth of their need of the gospel. Many will repent too late. They will weep and mourn at the remembrance of their sins. The burden of their guilt will be intolerable to them, but it will be *too late*. Many will believe too late. They will no longer be able to deny the reality of God, or the truth of his word. Like the devil, they will eventually believe and tremble. Many will desire forgiveness for the first time, but it will be too late.

The time is coming when all the values of the world will be turned upside down. Wealth, fame, luxury and all the other things which people live for today will become worthless. And the salvation preached in the gospel, which men despise today, will then be what men desire above all. But it will be too late: "Many will seek to enter and will not be able." Read for yourself the awful description of this in Proverbs 1:24-31.

Conclusion

I have tried to show you what the Lord Jesus meant by his words. Let me now try to apply the truth to your conscience.

22

1. Let me ask you a plain question, *Have you entered through the narrow gate or not?* I do not ask whether you believe in such a gate and hope one day to go through it. I ask you, Have you actually gone through it? Are you now inside it? If not, your sins are not forgiven; you are not born again; you are not fit for heaven; and when you die you will be eternally miserable. I plead with you now: think how short time is. Soon you will be gone. Soon it will be too late. The world will go on, but your body will be in the grave and your soul in hell. But today - today the gate stands before you, ready to open for you. God calls you. Jesus Christ is ready to save you. Only one thing is lacking, and that is that you should enter in.

2. Let me give some plain advice to all who are not inside the gate. *Enter it now, without delay.* No one ever got to heaven except through this gate. And no one (except those who die as infants) ever entered this gate without striving. But on the other hand, no one ever strove to enter and failed to get in. And no one ever entered and was afterwards sorry he had done so.

Since these things are true, you must seek Christ at once, and enter the gate while it is still open. Begin today. Go to the Lord Jesus in prayer. Confess to him your sinfulness. Keep nothing back. Cast yourself and all your spiritual concerns wholly upon him, and ask him to save you and put his Holy Spirit in you according to his promise. Why should you not do this? Thousands of people as bad as you have gone to Christ in this way, and none has been refused. And why should you not do so at once? Other people have experienced immediate repentance and conversion. The woman of Samaria came to the well a sinner and went away a new creature in Christ. The Philippian jailer became a disciple of the Lord Jesus in a single night. Why should you not give up your sins and lay hold of Christ this very day?

3. Finally, let me make a request to all who have entered the narrow gate. Will you *tell others* of the blessing which you have found? When Andrew was converted he immediately told his brother about Christ. Philip did the same with Nathaniel.

When Saul the Pharisee was converted, "Immediately he preached Christ in the synagogues, that he is the Son of God" (Acts 9:20). I long to see this kind of spirit among Christians today. Let us work while it is day, for "night is coming when no one can work" (John 9:4). The man who tries to show his neighbour the narrow gate is doing work of which God approves. Scripture says, "He who turns a sinner from the error of his way will save a soul from death" (James 5:20). Let us all waken up to a deeper sense of our responsibility in this matter. Are not many of those with whom we mix outside the narrow gate? Who can tell what a word may achieve, if it is spoken in faith and prayer? It may be the turning point in someone's history. Oh for more love and boldness among believers! "Many will seek to enter and will not be able." Who can think about such words and not be concerned about others?

3.
REALITY

"Rejected silver." - Jeremiah 6:30
"Nothing but leaves." - Mark 11:13
"Let us not love in word or in tongue, but in deed and in truth."
- 1 John 3:18
"You have a name that you are alive, but you are dead." -
Revelation 3:1

If we say we are Christians, let us make sure that our Christianity is *real*. Real Christianity is not something outward or temporary, but something inward, solid, living and lasting. We know the difference between solid gold and cheap tinsel, between what is real and what is imitation. Let us think of this as we think about our Christianity. Do you want your Christianity to give you comfort in this life and hope in death, and to stand the test of the Judgment of God? Then I ask you to stop to consider whether your Christianity is like solid gold or cheap tinsel.

1. Our Christianity must be real

I want to begin by showing you how important it is that your Christianity should be real. Perhaps you think there is little danger of its not being real. If so, you are wrong, for the Bible frequently reminds us of this very danger.

Look at the parables spoken by our Lord Jesus Christ. See how many of them point to the contrast between the real Christian and the merely outward Christian - for example the parables of the Sower, the Wheat and the Tares, the Wedding

Garment, and the Ten Virgins among others. (See Matthew 13:1-43, Matthew 22:1-14 and Matthew 25:1-13.) These show the danger of an outward Christianity that is not real.

Look at the language which our Lord Jesus Christ used about the scribes and Pharisees. Eight times in one chapter he denounced them as hypocrites in the most fearful language. (See Matthew 23.) By speaking so severely the Lord Jesus taught us how abominable unreality is in the sight of God.

Look at the startling fact that there is hardly one Christian grace which does not have a counterfeit described in God's Word. There is unreal *repentance*, for Saul, Ahab, Herod and Judas Iscariot had it, and were never saved. There is unreal *faith*, for Simon at Samaria had it, though his heart was not right in the sight of God. There is unreal *holiness*, for King Joash seemed very holy and good, but only as long as Jehoiada the priest was alive. There is unreal *love*, for the apostle John warns us, "Let us not love in word or in tongue, but in deed and in truth." There is unreal *praying*, for our Lord condemns the sin of the Pharisees who for a pretence made long prayers.

Surely all of this ought to make us think. What care we need to take to make sure that *our* Christianity is real!

2. Tests of reality

I want now to give you some tests by which you can test the reality of your Christianity. Don't just assume that everything is all right. Remember, this is a matter of eternal life or death.

Begin by asking yourself, What place does your Christianity occupy in your *heart*? It is not enough to believe the truth in your head, or to profess it with your lips, or even that it sometimes produces strong emotions within you. Real Christianity rules in the heart. It governs the affections, leads the will, directs the tastes and choices and decisions. Does *your* Christianity rule in your heart?

Secondly, ask yourself, What views of *sin* does your Christianity produce? Real Christianity, which the Holy Spirit

26

produces in the heart, will always lead to serious views of how bad sin is. You will not think of sin simply as something unfortunate which makes sinners the objects of pity, but as something abominable which God hates, and which makes the sinner guilty, lost and subject to God's just anger and condemnation. You will see sin as the cause of all the unhappiness in the world - the thing which has ruined God's good creation. Above all, you will see it as the thing which will ruin us eternally, unless our debt is paid and we are delivered from its bondage. Do you view sin like that?

Thirdly, ask yourself, What views of *Christ* does your Christianity produce? An unreal Christian may believe that Christ really existed and did good to men. He may show outward respect for Christ and attend Christian worship. But a real Christian will glory in Christ as the Redeemer, the Deliverer, the Great High Priest, the Friend, without whom he would have no hope at all. He will trust him, love him, delight in him, and draw comfort from him as the Mediator between God and men, and the One who is food, light, life and peace for his soul. Is this your view of Christ?

Fourthly, What *fruit* does your Christianity bear in your heart and life? Real Christianity is known by its fruits - the fruits of repentance, faith, hope, love, humility, spirituality, kindness, self- denial, forgiveness of others, self-control, truthfulness, and patience. The degree to which these are seen will vary from one believer to another, but the root of each of them is in every true child of God. Do *you* have these fruits?

Lastly, How do you feel about *the means of grace*, and what do you do about them? By the means of grace I mean those things which God has appointed to be the means of our spiritual growth. How do you feel about the Lord's Day? Is it a delight to you, a sweet foretaste of heaven to come? How do you feel about public worship, when the church comes together to pray and worship, to hear the Word of God preached and to sit at the Lord's Table? Are these important to you, or could you live without them? What about private prayer and Bible reading?

Are these a necessary part of your life? Do they bring you comfort, or do you find them tedious? Do you neglect them altogether? If these means of spiritual growth are not as necessary to your Christian life as food and drink are necessary to your body, you may well doubt whether your Christianity is real.

Conclusion

I appeal to you to test your Christianity by these five questions. If your Christianity is real, you have nothing to fear by facing them honestly. But if it is not, the sooner you discover this the better. You will have to face the question one day, for the Day of Judgment will test everything. If you face the truth *today*, you have time for repentance, but *then* it will be too late. Decide to face it now!

Let me conclude with a direct application of the truth to each reader.

1. I must speak a word of *warning* to those who know in their hearts that their Christianity is not real. Remember your danger, and how great your guilt is before God. God is the God of Truth. He hates all that is not true, and your Christianity is not true. Moreover, your unreal Christianity will fail you in the end. It will give you no comfort when it is most needed - in times of affliction, and on your deathbed. Above all it will fail you in the Day of Judgment.

2. I must speak a word of *advice* to those who are troubled in conscience by what they have read. Stop playing at Christianity! Stop treating Christianity as a game, and become an honest, wholehearted follower of the Lord Jesus Christ. Go to him today, and ask him to become your Saviour. Don't let your sinfulness keep you away. Remember he can take away any number of sins. But he does ask for reality. Put away all pretence, and come to him with all your heart and soul.

3. I must say a word of *encouragement* to all who have taken up the cross and are honest followers of Christ. I encourage you

to keep going, and not to be put off by any trials or difficulties. Never mind the opinions of others. Never be ashamed of being totally committed to the Lord Jesus. Men should indeed be ashamed of living for sin and for pleasure, but no one should be ashamed of living for Christ.

4. Finally, let us all remember that on the last day, nothing but reality will count. Remember the words of the Lord Jesus: "Many will say to me in that day, 'Lord, Lord, have we not prophesied in your name, cast out demons in your name, and done many wonders in your name?' And then I will declare to them, 'I never knew you; depart from me, you who practise lawlessness!'" (Matthew 7:22,23)

4.
PRAYER

"Men always ought to pray." - Luke 18:1
"I desire that the men pray everywhere." - 1 Timothy 2:8

Prayer is the most important subject in living the Christian life. Other things are very important - reading the Bible, observing the Lord's Day, attending church, hearing sermons and going to the Lord's Table. But none of these is as important as private prayer. I want to give you seven reasons why I say this, and I ask you to consider them very carefully.

1. Prayer is absolutely necessary

Prayer is absolutely necessary to our salvation. Of course I am not speaking about infants, but about those who call themselves Christians. No one who professes to be a Christian can be saved without praying. I hold as strongly as anyone that salvation is God's free gift. I would speak to the greatest sinner who ever lived, even if he were old and dying, and say, "Believe on the Lord Jesus Christ, even now, and you will be saved." But I cannot find that the Bible teaches that anyone will be saved without asking to be. Although nobody will be saved *by merit of* his prayers, nobody will be saved *without* prayer.

It is not absolutely necessary for salvation that someone should *read* the Bible. He may never have learned to read, or be blind, and yet have Christ. A deaf man, or someone who lives where the gospel is not preached, may be saved without *hearing* the gospel publicly preached. But *no one* can be saved without praying.

There are certain things which everyone must do for himself. Everybody has to attend to the needs of his own body and his own mind. Nobody else can do your eating, drinking or sleeping for you. And if you want to know something, nobody else can do your learning for you. And it is the same with your spiritual needs. Nobody else can repent for you. Nobody else can come to Christ for you. And nobody else can do your praying for you. *You yourself* must pray.

We get to know people in this world by speaking with them. If we don't speak to them we don't get to know them. Similarly we cannot get to know God without praying to him, and if we do not know him we certainly shall not be saved by him.

One day, heaven will be thronged with "a multitude which no one could number" (Revelation 7:9). But all these people will sing with one heart and one voice. Their experience will have been the same. *Each one* will have believed in Christ. *Each one* will have been washed in his blood. *Each one* will have been born again. And *each one* will have prayed. Unless we pray on earth we shall never praise in heaven.

In short, then, to be prayerless is to be without God, without Christ, without grace, without hope and without heaven. It is to be on the road to hell.

2. Prayer is one of the surest marks of a Christian

The habit of prayer is one of the surest marks of a true Christian. There is one respect in which all God's children on earth are alike. They all pray. The first sign of life in a new-born infant is that it breathes. In the same way the first act of the new-born Christian is to pray. Just as it is part of a child's nature to cry, so it is part of the Christian's nature to pray. He sees his need of mercy and grace. He feels his emptiness and weakness. Therefore he feels that he *must* pray.

31

I cannot find in the Bible even one of God's people who was not a man of prayer. It is characteristic of God's people that they "call on the Father" (1 Peter 1:17) and they "call on the Name of Jesus Christ our Lord" (1 Corinthians 1:2), whereas it is characteristic of the wicked that they "do not call on the Lord" (Psalm 14:4).

I have also read the lives of many outstanding Christians who have lived since the Bible was written. They have differed in all kinds of ways, but one thing they all have had in common: they have all been *people of prayer*.

I know quite well, of course, that a man may pray insincerely. The mere fact that a man prays proves nothing about his spiritual state, for he may simply be a hypocrite. But this I can say with certainty: *not* praying is a clear proof that a man is not yet a true Christian. Clearly he does not really feel his sins, or love God, or feel his debt of gratitude to Christ, or long to be holy. However much he may *talk* about religion, he cannot be a true Christian if he does not *pray*.

Let me also say that the habit of heart-felt private prayer is one of the best evidences that the Holy Spirit has really worked in a person's life. A man may preach or write books or do all l inds of other things from quite wrong motives, but a man will seldom get alone by himself and pour out his soul to God in private unless he is sincere. God himself has taught us that this is the best proof of a real conversion, for when he told Ananias to go to see Saul in Damascus, the only evidence he mentioned that Saul had undergone a real change of heart was this: "He is praying!" (Acts 9:11)

I know, of course, that many people come to faith slowly. They may go through many convictions, desires, feelings, resolves, hopes and fears. But all these things can come to nothing. A real heartfelt prayer, flowing from a broken and penitent spirit, is worth all these things put together. The first act when we have real faith will be to speak to God. Prayer is to faith what breath is to life. Just as we cannot live without breathing, so we cannot believe in Christ without praying.

3. Prayer is the most neglected Christian duty

No Christian duty is neglected as much as private prayer. I used to think that most people who call themselves Christians prayed. But I have come to a different conclusion now. I believe that the great majority who say they are Christians never pray at all. Prayer is a strictly private matter between God and us, which no-one else sees, and therefore there is a great temptation not to bother.

I believe that many *never say a single word of prayer at all*. They eat and drink, sleep and wake, live on God's earth and enjoy his mercies. They have bodies which must die, and they have the Day of Judgment and eternity ahead of them. Yet for all this they *never speak to God*. They live as though they were animals rather than men with never dying souls.

I believe that for many more, prayer is *nothing more than a form of words*. Some use set patterns of words without any sincere feeling for the things they say. Even when the pattern is a good one (like the Lord's Prayer) many rush through it without really thinking about it. We may be sure that God does not call this praying, even if *men* do. Prayer involves much more than words spoken with our lips. It involves our *hearts*, or it is not real prayer. No doubt Saul of Tarsus had said many long prayers before the Lord met him on the way to Damascus. But it was only when his heart had been broken that the Lord said, "He is praying!"

If you find all this very surprising, consider the following facts:

It is not *natural* to pray. The natural desire of our hearts is to get away from God. We do not naturally love him, but fear him. And by nature we have no sense of sin, or feeling of our spiritual needs, or faith in things we cannot see. We do not naturally desire to be holy. For these reasons, men do not naturally pray.

It is not *popular* to pray. All kinds of worldly activities are popular among men. But prayer is not popular, and many would do almost anything rather than admit publicly that they were in the habit of praying. In the light of these facts I believe that few people pray.

Consider also the lives that many people lead. When we see men plunging into sin, can we believe that they are praying constantly against sin? When we see men wholly taken up with the things of the world, can we think that they are regularly asking God for grace to serve him? How can they be, when they show no interest in him at all? Praying and sinning will never live together in the same heart. Prayer will choke sin, or sin will choke prayer. When I remember this and then look at men's lives, I believe that few people pray.

Consider also the deaths that many people die. Many dying people seem to be complete strangers to God. They lack the ability to speak to him. They give the distinct impression they have never really talked to him before. What I have seen for myself of dying people convinces me that few people pray.

4. We have great encouragements to pray

We have more encouragement to prayer than we have to any other Christian duty. God has done everything necessary to make prayer easy if only we will attempt it. He has provided for every difficulty, so that there is no excuse for us if we do not pray.

There is a *way* by which any man - however sinful and unworthy - may draw near to God the Father. Jesus Christ has opened that way by his sacrifice for us on the cross. God's holiness and justice need not frighten sinners away. Rather, let them cry to God in the name of Jesus. Let them plead the fact that his blood has made atonement for sin, and they will find God willing and ready to hear. The name of Jesus unfailingly ensures that God will hear our prayers. In his name we may draw near to God with boldness and pray with confidence. And God has promised to hear. Is this not a great encouragement to pray?

There is *an advocate* and *intercessor* always waiting to present the prayers of those who will make use of him. He presents our prayers before the throne of God. Our prayers are feeble in themselves, but when presented by the Lord Jesus they are effective. And his ear is always open to the cry of all those who want mercy and grace. Is this not a great encouragement to pray?

There is the *Holy Spirit* who is always ready to help us in prayer, for this is one part of his office (Romans 8:26). He is the "Spirit of grace and supplication" (Zechariah 12:10). We have only to seek his assistance.

There are great and precious *promises* to those who pray. Read Matthew 7:7,8 and 21:22; John 14:13,14; Luke 11:5-13 and 18:1-8. Think over these passages, for they contain the greatest possible encouragements to pray.

There are wonderful *examples* in Scripture of the power of prayer. Prayer opened the Red Sea; it brought water from the rock; it made the sun stand still. Things which were impossible by any other means were done by prayer.

What greater encouragements could you look for than these things? Or what greater folly could there be than to neglect prayer in spite of all this encouragement?

5. Prayer is the secret of holiness

Diligence in prayer is the secret of eminent holiness. Without doubt there is a great deal of difference between the achievements of true Christians. How much more progress some make than others! Some who are truly converted seem to remain spiritual babies all their lives. From one year to another they do not seem to grow. They are troubled by the same besetting sins; they still need the milk of the Word rather than strong meat; their spiritual interests remain narrow and confined to their own little circle. But there are others who are always growing - always advancing in the Christian life. They grow in faith; they grow in good works; they attempt great things and do

35

great things. When they fail, they try again; when they fall, they soon rise again. They think of themselves as poor and unprofitable servants, yet they are the people whose lives commend the Christian faith to others.

Now, how can we explain this difference among the Lord's people? Why are some so much holier than others? I believe the difference in nineteen cases out of twenty arises from different habits about private prayer. I believe that those who are not eminently holy pray only a little, while those who are eminently holy pray a great deal. I believe that once someone is converted to God, whether or not he becomes eminently holy depends chiefly on his diligence in the use of those means which God has appointed. And the main means by which believers have advanced in holiness is the habit of diligent private prayer. Read the lives of great servants of God and you will see that this is true. No Christian became a great Christian without becoming a man of prayer. If you wish to grow as a Christian, you must learn the value of private prayer.

6. The neglect of prayer causes backsliding

Neglect of prayer is one great cause of backsliding. It is possible to go *backwards* in the Christian life, after making a good start. The Galatian Christians progressed well for a time, and then turned aside after false teachers. Peter loudly proclaimed his love for the Lord, but in a time of trial denied him. And to be a backslider is miserable. It is one of the worst things that can happen to a man. I know that real grace in a man cannot be destroyed. I know that true union with Christ cannot be broken. But I believe that a man may fall away so far that he loses sight of his Christian standing and despairs of his own salvation. And this is the nearest thing to hell. A wounded conscience, a mind sick of itself, a memory full of self-reproach, a heart pierced through with the Lord's arrows, a spirit broken with a load of inward accusation - all this is a *taste of hell*. Consider the solemn words, "The backslider in heart shall be filled with his own ways" (Proverbs 14:14).

Now, what is the cause of most backsliding? I believe it is generally caused by neglect of private prayer. It is my considered opinion, and I repeat it, that backsliding generally begins with *neglect of private prayer*.

Prayerlessness in daily life and decision-making has led many Christians into a condition of spiritual paralysis, or to the point where God has allowed them to fall badly into sin.

We may be sure that men fall in private long before they fall in public. Like Peter, they first neglect the Lord's warning to watch and pray, and then, like Peter, their strength is gone and when temptation comes they fall into sin. The world then takes notice of their fall, and scoffs. But the world does not recognise the real reason, which is prayerlessness.

If you are a Christian, you who are reading this book, I hope you never become a backslider. But if you wish to avoid this, *be careful about your praying*.

7. Prayer obtains happiness and contentment

Prayer is one of the surest ways of obtaining happiness and contentment. This world is a world of sorrow. Ever since sin entered it, it has been impossible for anyone completely to escape sorrows of one kind or another. Now the best way to cope with this is by *taking everything to God in prayer*. In the Old Testament we read, "Cast your burden on the Lord, and he shall sustain you" (Psalm 55:22). In the New Testament we read, "Be anxious for nothing, but in everything by prayer and supplication, with thanksgiving, let your requests be made known to God; and the peace of God, which surpasses all understanding, will guard your hearts and minds through Christ Jesus" (Philippians 4:6,7). This has been the practice of God's people in all ages. When Jacob was in great fear of his brother Esau, he prayed (Genesis 32:22-32). When Paul and Silas were thrown into prison at Philippi, they prayed (Acts 16:23-25). The only way to be truly happy in a world like this is always to be casting our cares on God. When Christians fail to do this, and try instead to bear their own burdens, they become unhappy.

If only we will go to him, the Lord Jesus is always waiting to hear and help us. He knows all about the trials and sorrows of this world, for he lived in it for more than thirty years. And he can make us truly happy - whatever our outward condition - if we trust and call on him. Prayer can lighten the heaviest cross. Prayer can bring light into our darkness. Prayer can bring comfort in the greatest sorrow and loneliness. I want everyone who reads this book to be a really happy Christian. But if you are to be happy there is no more important duty for you to attend to than that of prayer.

Conclusion

Let me close with some advice to various classes of reader.

1. Let me speak to *those who do not pray*. Prayerless friend, I must warn you of your danger. If you die as you are, you will be lost. You are completely without excuse, for you cannot give even one good reason why you should live without prayer. Do not say that you *do not know how* to pray. Prayer is simply speaking to God. You need no education to pray - only the desire to do so. The tiniest infant can cry when he is hungry. If you are conscious of your need you will soon find something to say to God. Do not say you *have no place in which to pray*. Anyone can find an adequate place if he really wants to. Do not say you *have no time to pray*. You have plenty of time, if only you are prepared to use it aright. Daniel had to deal with the affairs of a great empire, but he still prayed three times a day (Daniel 6:10). Do not say you *cannot pray till you have been born again and have faith*. If you lack these things you must cry out to God for them. "Seek the LORD while he may be found; call upon him while he is near" (Isaiah 55:6). Do not put it off. Salvation is very near you *today*. Do not miss it because you will not ask.

2. Let me speak to *those who desire to be saved* but do not know what to do. I advise you to go right now to the Lord Jesus Christ, in the nearest private place you can find, and beg him in prayer to save you. Tell him that you have heard that he receives sinners, and has said, "The one who comes to me I will by no means cast out." Tell him you are a lost sinner, and that you come to him on the strength of his own invitation. Tell him that you are entirely in his hands: that unless he saves you there is no hope for you at all. Ask him to deliver you from the guilt, the power and the consequences of your sins. Ask him to forgive you, to give you a new heart, to put his Holy Spirit in you. Ask him to enable you to become his disciple and servant from this day and for ever. Do all this today if you have any concern about your soul. Remember that he is willing to save you, for you are a sinner and he came into the world to save sinners (Luke 5:32, 1 Timothy 1:15). Do not stay away because you feel unworthy. The more ill you are, the more you need a doctor. You would not stay away from the doctor because you were too ill. Don't worry about the kind of language you use. Jesus will understand you. And don't despair because you do not seem to get an immediate answer. He is listening. Keep on praying, and the answer will come. If you desire to be saved, remember what I have told you and act upon it, and you will certainly be saved.

3. Finally, let me speak to *those who do pray*. Let nothing at all discourage you. You may often feel great discouragement. Your times of prayer may be times of conflict. But this is quite common, for the devil hates to see you pray. So you must go on. Let me then offer you some words of brotherly advice about your prayers.

Remember the importance of *reverence* and *humility* in prayer. Think of who God is, and who you are.

Remember the need you have of *the Holy Spirit's help* in prayer, and be careful not to let your praying become a mere formality.

Remember how important it is to pray *regularly*. You must see prayer as one of the most important activities of each day, and time for prayer must be built into your daily routine.

Remember the importance of *persevering* in prayer. You will often be tempted to neglect your prayers, or to cut them very short. This always comes from the devil, no matter how plausible the reasons for doing so might seem.

Be *earnest* in prayer. It is "fervent" prayer which achieves much (James 5:16).

Remember the importance of *praying with faith*. We must believe that if we ask according to God's will our prayers will be answered (Mark 11:24). You must expect answers to your prayers.

Consider the importance of *boldness* in your prayers. I do not mean an improper familiarity, but arguing with God on the basis of his own Word and promise.

Remember the importance of *asking God for much*. How often is it true of believers that they "do not have because they do not ask" (James 4:2).

Be *specific* in prayer. Confess your specific sins; pray for your specific weaknesses; tell God your specific needs.

Remember the importance of *praying for others*. Beware of letting your prayers become narrow and self-centred.

Be *thankful* in prayer. We have much to be thankful for, and I dare not call any prayer a true prayer if thankfulness has no part in it.

Finally, let me remind you of the need for *watchfulness over your prayers*. True Christian experience begins in prayer; it flourishes in prayer; and it decays with the neglect of prayer. Prayer is a kind of spiritual pulse - by it you may know whether you are spiritually healthy. Be watchful over your prayer life, and I shall be very surprised if anything goes very seriously wrong with your spiritual progress.

5.
BIBLE READING

"From childhood you have known the Holy Scriptures, which are able to make you wise for salvation through faith which is in Christ Jesus." - 2 Timothy 3:15
"You are mistaken, not knowing the Scriptures." - Matthew 22:29

Next to prayer, Bible reading is the most important Christian duty. The Bible is "able to make us wise for salvation through faith which is in Christ Jesus" (2 Timothy 3:15). By reading it we can learn what we should believe, what we should be, and what we should do. We can learn how to live with spiritual comfort, and how to die in spiritual peace. Happy is the man who not only reads the Bible, but also obeys it and makes it the standard of his faith and practice! Let me give you eight plain reasons why everyone who cares about his salvation should prize the Bible, study it regularly and become thoroughly familiar with what it says.

1. There is no other book like the Bible

There is no other book in existence which was written like the Bible. The Bible is completely different from any other book - it was inspired by God (2 Timothy 3:16). God taught the writers of it what to say, putting thoughts and ideas into their minds, and guiding their pens to write them down. When you read the Bible you are reading the words of God himself. From beginning to end the Bible is the Word of God, and it alone is absolutely perfect.

I shall not waste time trying to prove the inspiration of the Bible. The book itself is its own best witness. It is the greatest standing miracle in the world, and nothing but divine inspiration can account for it.

We know, of course, that different writers of the Bible write in their own different styles - Isaiah writes differently from Jeremiah, and Paul writes differently from John. But this is only like a man playing on different musical instruments - his breath will produce different sounds according to whether he is playing a flute or a pipe or a trumpet, but it is the same breath that produces each sound. In the same way it is God himself who inspired each and every one of the human writers of the Bible, so that every chapter, every verse and every word is from God. If only people who are troubled with questions about the Bible would take and read it for themselves! How many problems and objections would disappear immediately! And how many people would discover God for themselves in his book! How important it is, then, that *you* should read the Bible!

2. The Bible tells us all we need to know for salvation

Everything you need to know to be saved is found in the Bible. We live in days when human knowledge has increased enormously. Education is more widespread than at any time in history. This is good, but we must remember that if we have the best education possible and yet do not know the truths revealed in the Bible, we shall not be saved from hell. Remember, a man may have an amazing knowledge of every kind of subject, and not be saved. Death brings an end to all human achievements. On the other hand a man may be quite ignorant and illiterate and yet be saved. If he has heard the great truths of the Bible with his ears, and believed them in his heart, his soul will be saved. Knowing the truths of the Bible is more important by far than any other sphere of knowledge.

3. The Bible deals with matters of greater importance than any other book

No other book contains matters of such importance as the Bible. It is the Bible which tells us God's great plan of salvation, and the way in which our sins can be forgiven. Without the Bible, we should know nothing of the coming of the Lord Jesus into the world to save sinners, nothing of his dying in our place - the righteous in the place of the unrighteous - nothing of the justification of every sinner who believes in Jesus, nothing of the willingness of the Father, Son and Holy Spirit to save even the worst of men.

It is the Bible which tells us about the life and character of the Lord Jesus Christ - the great Mediator between God and men. Four separate witnesses record his ministry and his miracles. They tell us about his life and teaching, his death and resurrection, his power, love, kindness and patience. They tell us about these things so plainly that no-one can fail to understand them.

The Bible also tells us about the lives of good people. Many were people just like us with all our problems. The Bible does not attempt to hide their mistakes and their weaknesses. It reminds us that the Saviour of these people is ready to be our Saviour too. The Bible also contains many important warnings drawn from the lives of bad people, to remind us that the God who punished their sins will punish us as well if we cling to our sins. The Bible contains many precious promises to encourage those who love God. It gives us deep insight into the character of man.

Where else could we learn about all these things? How important that we should read the Bible!

4. The Bible produces more wonderful effects than any other book

No other book has ever produced such a wonderful effect on men as the Bible. This is the book whose teaching "turned the

43

world upside down" (Acts 17:6) in the days of the Apostles. The Apostles were a handful of men sent out to challenge the superstition, false religion and immorality of the world. They had no worldly weapons to force their message on anyone, and no riches to bribe anyone to believe. But they were armed with this book, and in a few generations they completely changed the condition of society.

In the days of the Reformation, this book transformed Europe. Six hundred years ago, great darkness covered the Christian church. A great change had come over Christianity, so that it was hardly recognisable any more. Then men began to translate the Bible into the languages of the people, and the church was transformed again. Similar things have happened at other times. What great wickedness existed in Israel in the days of its kings! But this is not surprising, since the law of the Lord had been lost, thrown aside in a corner of the temple, until it was found in the days of Josiah (2 Kings 22:8).

The Bible has brought great blessing to nations where its message has been widely received. It has led to good laws, to higher standards of morality, to the great blessing of the Sabbath Day, to the founding of compassionate institutions for the sick, the poor, old people and orphans. These have seldom been found in countries which have not had the Bible.

5. The Bible does more than any other book for its readers

No book can do so much for those who read it properly as the Bible can. The Bible deals with matters far more important than how to succeed in this present life. It deals with matters of eternal life. The Bible is "able to make you wise for salvation through faith which is in Christ Jesus". It can show you the way to heaven. It can teach you everything you need to know and believe, and everything you need to do to be saved. It can show you yourself - a sinner. It can show you God - in all his holiness. And it can show you the Lord Jesus Christ, who alone can reconcile you to God.

44

It is the Bible which the Holy Spirit uses to convert sinners. He brings its truth home to their conscience and through the truth he works a moral miracle in their lives. Day by day throughout the world all kinds of people are experiencing this miracle of the new birth brought about by the Holy Spirit through the Bible.

The Bible is the chief means by which Christians grow after they have been converted. The Holy Spirit uses his own Word, either as it is read privately or as it is preached publicly, to cleanse and sanctify them, to instruct them in righteousness, and to equip them for all good works. (See Psalm 119:9; John 17:17; 2 Timothy 3:16,17.) The Bible can show you how to live your everyday life in a way that pleases God. It can teach you to endure hardship and even persecution, and to think about death and the coming judgment without fear. It can awaken you when you are spiritually drowsy. It can comfort you when you are sad. It can bring you back when you are going astray. It can give you strength when you are weak. It can keep you from evil when you are with others, and it can speak to you when you are alone. It can do all these things even for the most insignificant Christian. If the Holy Spirit is living in your heart and you have the Bible in your hand, you have everything that is absolutely necessary for your Christian life. Even if you were put in prison and cut off completely from other Christians, you would have in your possession God's infallible guide for life.

Some people complain that the Bible contains many things that are hard to understand. This is perfectly true, but it is no reason to stop reading it. The fault lies in our understanding, not in the Bible itself, and it is only as we continue to read it that we shall understand it more. We certainly must not be deterred by the hard things, for there are also many things which are perfectly clear and easy. The great truths which we must understand in order to be saved are plain for all who desire to know them. It would be extremely foolish to ignore what we can understand because of the parts which are difficult.

Other people complain that not everyone who reads the Bible gets from it the benefits I have been speaking about. The answer is simple: those who do not benefit from reading the Bible are not reading it the right way. The Bible must be read with humility and with prayer or we cannot expect it to do us any good. No one who reads the Bible with a child-like and persevering spirit will ever miss the way to heaven. God's Word is strictly true when it says that "if you incline your ear to wisdom, and apply your heart to understanding; yes, if you cry out for discernment, and lift up your voice for understanding, if you seek her as silver and search for her as for hidden treasures, then you will understand the fear of the LORD, and find the knowledge of God" (Proverbs 2:2-5).

6. The Bible is the standard of Christian doctrine and duty

The Bible is the only standard by which all questions about doctrine or Christian duty can be decided. God knows that his children need to have an infallible standard of what is true and what is right, and he has graciously given us just that in the Bible. We should be extremely grateful for this, because there is so much confusion in the world both about Christian doctrine and about Christian practice.

There is much confusion about Christian *doctrine*. Different churches give different answers even to the most important questions about the Christian faith. Roman Catholics and Protestants, Evangelicals and Liberals, Mormons and Jehovah's Witnesses all claim to have the truth, yet what one teaches is totally different from what another says. How can anybody find the truth when things are so confusing? There is only one answer. God himself has given us an infallible standard of truth in the Bible. We must take it as our standard. We must believe nothing which is not in accord with the Bible. It does not matter who says that something is true. It does not matter what his status in the church may be. What he says must be tested by the Bible. A man may be a Christian minister or pastor. But still what he says must be tested by the Bible. If he is a true minister he will be very happy for you to do this. Indeed, he will encourage you to read the Bible and to check for yourself whether his teaching is true. Only a false teacher will ask you to believe on his own authority or on the authority of his church. The aim of every true minister is always to help you to see the truth for yourself in the Word of God.

There is also much confusion about Christian *practice*. Every Christian who really desires to do what is pleasing to God will have to make decisions about all kinds of practical questions. He will be confronted with questions relating to his daily work. Probably there will be certain things which almost everybody does, but which do not seem to him to be quite right. And away from work there are sure to be questions about how to spend his time. Many people engage in forms of entertainment which raise questions as to whether they are wise and right. And there will be questions relating to his family life. What standards of behaviour should apply here? Is something all right just because other people who call themselves Christians are doing it?

Again there can be only one answer to all these questions. The Bible must be our standard. Whenever we are confronted with a question about Christian practice, we must apply the teaching of the Bible. Sometimes the Bible will deal with it directly, and we must go by its direct teaching. Often the Bible will not deal with it directly, and then we must look for general *principles* to guide us. It does not matter what other people think. Their behaviour is not a standard for us. But the Bible is a standard for us, and it is by the Bible that we must live.

7. God's true servants have always loved the Bible and lived on its teachings

The Bible is the book which all true servants of God have always lived on and loved. Every living creature needs food. When a sinner becomes a new creature in Christ Jesus, he needs spiritual food. That food is the Word of God. Just as a new-born child desires its mother's milk, so every truly converted person loves God's Word. So if someone despises Bible reading, or thinks little of Bible preaching, I regard it as quite certain that he is not yet born again.

The Old Testament believers loved God's Word - consider Job 23:12 and Psalm 119:97. The Apostles loved God's Word, for they and their companions were men "mighty in the Scriptures". The Lord Jesus himself loved the Word. He read it publicly. He quoted it continually. He used it as his weapon against the devil. He said repeatedly, "The Scripture must be fulfilled." Almost the last thing he did on earth was to "open the understanding of his disciples, that they might understand the Scriptures" (Luke 24:45).

Throughout Christian history, God's people have loved his Word. All those whom God has used in the work of his kingdom have loved it. Wherever the gospel has gone, educated and uneducated people alike have learned to love God's Word. This is something they have in common, even when they disagree about questions of church organisation and other such matters. When all God's people are finally gathered together in heaven, they will find that they have all been through the same experiences. They will all have been born of God's Spirit and pardoned through Christ's blood. And they will all have loved the Word of God and made it their food and delight during their pilgrimage on earth.

Let me ask you again, What are *you* doing with God's Word?

8. It is only the Bible which can comfort a dying man

The Bible is the only book which can comfort a man when he is dying. Death is a solemn event which comes to us all. It marks the end of every opportunity for repentance, and is the door either to heaven or to hell. Even for the Christian believer,

48

death is solemn. In death he is safe, for he belongs to Christ, but it is still solemn. We naturally shrink from it. To part from those we love to go into another world is not easy. It makes sense, then, for everyone to think calmly about how he is going to meet death when it comes. Let me tell you something about it.

The best things in this world cannot comfort a dying man. Money can buy him the best medical attention, but it cannot buy him peace of heart and conscience. Relatives and friends cannot comfort him either. They can do their very best for his needs, but they cannot help his inward fears and troubled conscience. Books and newspapers cannot comfort him. However much he may have enjoyed them in life, in death they will be nothing to him. But there is one book which is a source of comfort, and that book is the Bible. Chapters of the Bible, verses from the Bible, truths drawn from the Bible - these are a man's only chance of comfort when he is dying. Of course, I cannot say that it will necessarily do him any good if he has never valued the Bible before. I have seen too many death-beds to say that. I do not say whether the man who has neglected the Bible all his life is likely to get comfort from it in his death. But I do say that no dying man will get any real comfort anywhere else.

I say that this truth applies to everyone without exception. It applies to kings as well as to the poor. It applies to the best educated as well as to the unlearned. I tell you plainly, that although people seem to live comfortably without the Bible, not one of them will die comfortably without it. I have seen many people die, some with and some without comfort in death. But one thing I have never seen. I have never seen anyone enjoy real, solid, rational peace on his death-bed, who did not get it from the Bible. This is the book I am writing to you about, and I ask you for the last time, What are *you* doing with the Bible?

Conclusion

Let me close by speaking plainly to the consciences of different kinds of people who may be reading this book.

1. Perhaps you can read, but *never read the Bible at all*. If this is your condition, I can speak no words of comfort to you, for you are in danger of losing your soul. Your neglect of the Bible is plain proof that you do not love God. A man with a healthy body has a healthy appetite, and a man with a healthy soul has an appetite for God's Word. But *you* are obviously suffering a terrible spiritual disease. Will you not repent?

I know I cannot reach your heart, to make you see and feel these things, but I protest against your neglect of the Bible and I appeal to your conscience to consider my protest. Don't leave it too late to repent! Don't put off reading the Bible till you are dying and then find that it means nothing to you when you need it most! Don't go on saying, "People do perfectly well without all this Bible reading." You will find to your cost that people do very badly, and end in hell. Be careful you don't one day have to say, "If only I had paid as much attention to the Bible as I did to other books and magazines and newspapers, I would not have been left without hope in my last hours of life." I have given you a plain warning: may God have mercy on your soul.

2. Perhaps you are willing to begin reading the Bible but you *need advice about it*. Let me try to help you.

Begin reading your Bible today. Good intentions are not enough. You must actually begin to read. - Read the Bible with an earnest desire to understand it. Reading without understanding will do you no good. - Read the Bible with childlike faith and humility. You must submit to it, not sit in judgment upon it. - Read the Bible with the intention to obey it, applying it to yourself. It must affect the way you live your life. - Read the Bible every day. You like to eat food daily, and the Bible is the food of your soul. - Read the whole Bible, and read it systematically. You have no right only to read your favourite

50

portions. - Interpret the Bible in a simple, straightforward manner. The simplest and most obvious interpretation is normally the correct one. - Read the Bible with Christ constantly in mind. Even in reading the Old Testament, try to understand how it points forward to him.

I firmly believe that if you will act upon these principles God will not let you misunderstand the way to heaven.

3. Perhaps you are someone who loves and believes the Bible, yet you *don't read it very much*. You are likely to get little comfort from the Bible in times of need. And you are likely never to become firmly grounded in the truth. Moreover you are likely to make big mistakes in life - in your marriage, family life, relationships with others. And you are likely to be misled, at least for a time, by false teachers. It is not enough for you to read the Bible a little - you must read it a great deal. You must "let the Word of Christ dwell in you richly" (Colossians 3:16).

4. Perhaps you are someone who reads the Bible a lot, but you are *tempted to give up because you think it is doing you no good*. Let me tell you that this temptation comes from the devil. The Bible may be doing you more good than you realise. It may be having an unseen effect upon your character, and keeping you back from sins and errors which you would otherwise fall into. If you stop reading it you may discover this to your cost!

5. Perhaps you *really love the Bible, live on it and read it a great deal*. If so, then resolve to read the Bible more each year you live - to get it into your memory and your heart. When you are dying you may be unable to read it, and it will be precious then to have it hidden in your heart (Psalm 119:11). Resolve too to be even more watchful over your habits of Bible reading each year you live, and to honour the Bible more in your family life. Resolve to meditate more on the Bible, and to talk more to other believers about it. Finally, resolve to live by the Bible more and more. Let it be the test of everything you do, and be determined with God's help to be governed by it.

6.
LOVE

"And now abide faith, hope, love, these three; but the greatest of these is love." - *1 Corinthians 13:13*

Love is the highest Christian grace. Everyone professes to admire it. Many admit they know nothing about Christian doctrine, but profess to understand and possess Christian love. But many have false ideas about love which need to be put right. Indeed, many misunderstand it completely. I want to speak plainly about it, for the truth is that there is nothing in the world more scarce than Christian love.

1. The importance of love

I want you to see, first of all, what an important place the Bible gives to love. Look for yourself at these passages of Scripture - 1 Corinthians 13:1-3; Colossians 3:14; 1 Timothy 1:5; 1 Peter 4:8; John 13:34-35; Matthew 25:41-46; Romans 13:8; Ephesians 5:2; 1 John 4:7,8. These verses need no comment from me. They show how immensely important Christian love is in God's sight.

2. What love is

Let me show you, secondly, what the love spoken of in the Bible really is, and what it is not. I begin with what it is not.

Love is not just giving to the poor. Paul says plainly that someone may "bestow all his goods to feed the poor"(1 Corinthians 13:3) and not have love. Care for the poor is an undeniable Christian duty, but we may do it and still be completely lacking in Christian love.

Love does not mean that we never condemn anybody's behaviour. The verse, "Do not judge" does not mean you are not to disapprove of things that are wrong. Biblical love does not mean we are to ignore sin or to speak well of immorality.

Biblical love does not mean that we should never disapprove of anyone's religious opinions. Biblical love does not say that everyone is going to heaven and nobody to hell, or that everyone is right and nobody is wrong. True love says, "Do not believe every spirit, but test the spirits, whether they are of God, because many false prophets have gone out into the world" (1 John 4:1).

Let us now consider what love is. First, it is love to *God*. Whoever has this love wants to love God with all his heart, soul, mind and strength. Secondly, it is love to *man*. Whoever has this love will want to love his neighbour as himself. Biblical love will show in a Christian's actions, making him ready to do good to everyone, without looking for any reward. It will show itself in willingness to bear evil. It will make him patient when provoked, forgiving, meek and humble. He will often deny himself for the sake of peace and will be more interested in promoting peace than in securing his own rights. Biblical love will show in a Christian's general attitude. He will be kind, unselfish, good-tempered and considerate, gentle and courteous, thoughtful of others' comfort, concerned for others' feelings and more willing to give than to receive. True love never envies, and never rejoices in people's troubles.

The perfect pattern of this love is found in the life of the Lord Jesus Christ. Jesus was hated, persecuted and criticised but he endured patiently. He was always kind and patient to everyone. Yet he exposed wickedness and rebuked those who sinned. He denounced false doctrine and false practices. He spoke as freely of hell as of heaven. He showed that perfect love does not approve of everybody's life or opinions, and that it is possible to condemn evil and still be full of love.

This, then, is what true Christian love is. But how little of it there is in the earth even among Christians! How happy the world would be if only there were more real biblical love!

3. Where love comes from

Let me show you, thirdly, where biblical love comes from. It is certainly not natural to man. Naturally we are all selfish, envious, unkind, and ill-tempered. We see this even in children, for by nature the human heart knows nothing of true love. True love will only be found in a heart that has been changed and renewed by the Holy Spirit. But when we become "partakers of the divine nature" (2 Peter 1:4) by union with Christ, one of the first features of that new nature is Christian love.

Such a heart will be convinced of the sinfulness of selfishness and lack of love and will fight against these things. It will also feel a debt of gratitude to the Lord Jesus who died for us, and will desire to be like him in love. The love of Christ poured out in our hearts by the Holy Spirit is the surest source of Christian love.

I ask you take special note of what I am saying here. You cannot have the fruit of Christianity without the roots. You cannot have Christian love without conversion, repentance and faith, and union with Christ. Real love comes down from above. It is the fruit of the Spirit. If you desire Christian love, you must get it from Christ.

4. Love is the greatest of the graces

Let me show you, lastly, why the apostle Paul in 1 Corinthians 13:13 calls love the greatest of the graces. Now Paul often speaks about how important faith is, for it is by faith that we come to Christ and are saved. By faith we are justified and have peace with God. But here Paul says that love is even greater than faith!

54

We are not to think for a moment that love can atone for our sins or get us peace with God. Only Christ can do that, and it is faith alone which unites us to Christ. Nor does Paul mean that love can exist without faith, for the one cannot exist without the other. But there are three reasons why love is greater than faith or hope.

First, God himself is full of love. God has no need of either faith or hope, but "God is love." Therefore, love in a Christian makes him like God. Secondly, love is the most useful grace to others. Faith and hope are of great personal benefit, but it is love which makes a Christian useful to others. Thirdly, love will last forever. It will never die. In heaven, everyone will be full of love. Faith will give way to sight, and hope will give way to full experience. But love will last for ever.

Conclusion

Let me close with a question and an exhortation.

1. The question is a simple one, but of great importance. *Do you have love?* Without it, you are nothing. Without it, you lack the mark of being a disciple of Jesus. Do not be content with a head knowledge of the truth. Do not be content with thinking you have faith. True faith is always accompanied by love. Examine your daily life, your attitudes to others, the way you speak. Do you treat others lovingly at all times - even when provoked? I appeal to you not to rest till you know real love in your heart. Ask the Lord Jesus to teach you how to love. Ask him to put his Holy Spirit in you and change your nature. Happy is the man or woman who really "walks in love".

2. My exhortation is directed towards those who do know real love in their hearts. First, *practise love*. Love grows by being exercised. Let love control your whole life - not only the big things, but the small things too. Secondly, *teach love to others*. Teach others the importance of kindness, helpfulness and being considerate. Teach them *"above all things* to put on love" (Colossians 3:14).

55

7.
ZEAL

"It is good to be zealous in a good thing always." - Galatians 4:18

The Bible requires Christians to be zealous people. Christ gave himself that we might be "zealous for good works" (Titus 2:14). He said to the church at Laodicea, "Be zealous and repent" (Revelation 3:19). In this chapter I want to show you the importance of Christian zeal, and to encourage you to be a zealous Christian.

1. What Christian zeal is

Christian zeal is a burning desire to please God, to do his will and to advance his glory in the world. No one feels this desire by nature, but God's Spirit puts it in the heart of every believer when he is converted. In some believers this desire is much stronger than in others. When it is really strong, a man will make any sacrifice, go through any trouble, deny himself anything, give all his energies and even his life itself, if only he can please God and honour Christ.

A zealous man *lives for one thing alone*. His whole life is given over to one pursuit, and that is to please God. It does not matter to him what the personal consequences may be, or what men may think. His zeal will always show itself, whatever his circumstances. If he cannot be outwardly active in serving Christ, he will give himself to prayer. If he cannot do a work himself, he will give the Lord no rest till he raises up someone else to do it.

We all know the mental attitude which makes men great in the world. They put aside everything except what they are striving for, and aim constantly at that one thing. It is like that in the realm of science. It is like that with men who make huge fortunes. And when the same mental outlook is consecrated to Christ, that is what is meant by Christian zeal.

Zeal was *characteristic of all the apostles*. Consider the apostle Paul. When he spoke to the elders at Ephesus for the last time he said, "But none of these things move me, nor do I count my life dear to myself" (Acts 20:24). He wrote to the Philippians, "One thing I do ... I press towards the goal for the prize of the upward call of God in Christ Jesus" (Philippians 3:13,14). From the day of his conversion he gave up all his earthly prospects, left everything for Christ's sake, and went throughout the world preaching the Christ whom he had once despised. He suffered hardship, persecution, oppression, imprisonment and eventually death itself for Christ's sake. This was true Christian zeal.

Zeal was *characteristic of the early Christians*. Many lost everything in the world for Christ's sake. Their faith brought them persecution and reproach, and their sufferings proved that they were in earnest.

Zeal has been *characteristic of men of God throughout history*. Martin Luther and the Reformers were zealous. They were ready to lay down their lives for Christ. Missionaries like William Carey and Henry Martyn were zealous. Martyn was a brilliant man, with the prospect of dazzling success in his chosen profession, but he chose instead to preach Christ in heathen lands.

Zeal was *characteristic of the Lord Jesus Christ himself.* If we began to give examples of his zeal, we would never end! He was *all zeal*.

In the light of these things, we must never despise Christian zeal!

2. The characteristics of true Christian zeal

It is important that we should understand what *kind* of zeal we are to have. Many people think that so long as someone is sincere, his zeal must be right. But that is not true, as we shall see.

True zeal must be *according to knowledge*, that is, enlightened by God's Word. The Jews who persecuted the early church had great zeal, but it was *not* "according to knowledge" (Romans 10:2). Peter had zeal when he cut off Malchus' ear, but his zeal was unenlightened. The followers of false religions are often very zealous, but it is not in accord with the truth.

True zeal must *spring from true motives*. The zeal of the Pharisees sprang from party-spirit. Some men's zeal springs from selfishness - they are out for what they can gain for themselves. Some men's zeal springs from love of praise. But God examines our hearts, and true zeal must spring from the love of God and desire for his glory.

True zeal will be concerned with *things which God himself is concerned about*. We should be zealous to be holy (Philippians 3:13,14). We should be zealous for the salvation of the lost (1 Corinthians 9:22). We should be zealous in opposing everything which God hates, and zealous in maintaining the doctrines of the gospel (Galatians 2:11).

True zeal will be *mingled with love*. It will not be bitter or harsh. It will hate the sin, but love the sinner. It will hate wickedness, yet be ready to do good to evil men. Jesus exposed false teachers, yet wept over Jerusalem. Paul earnestly rebuked the errors of the Galatians, yet cared for them like little children (Galatians 4:19).

True zeal will be *joined with deep humility*. When Moses came down from the mount, he did not know that his face shone. In the same way, the truly zealous man is more likely to mourn over what he has failed to achieve than to boast about his zeal!

I appeal to you to think about these characteristics of true Christian zeal. Remember that a man may be sincerely zealous, yet completely wrong. Make sure that *your* zeal is in accord with God's Word!

3. Why it is good to have Christian zeal

True zeal is good, because it benefits the Christian himself, the church, and society generally.

Zeal is beneficial *to the Christian personally*. Just as exercise is good for our bodily health, so zeal is good for our spiritual health. Those who are zealous for Christ are likely to know more than others of inner joy, peace, comfort and happiness. Those who strive the most for God's glory are likely to be honoured the most by God.

Zeal is beneficial *to the church corporately*. It is impossible to overestimate the debt the church owes to men of zeal. Men with lesser gifts but with great zeal have often done more for the church than men with greater gifts but less zeal. Even one truly zealous person in a church can achieve much, for zeal is contagious. One truly zealous man can awaken and stir up others, and do much good.

Zeal is beneficial *to society*. Evangelism and good works are inspired by it. Without men of Christian zeal the world must perish. But zealous men are ready to go into the world to preach the gospel and do good wherever they can.

If you are a Christian, be careful not to quench Christian zeal. Try to stir it up within yourself, and be careful not to oppose it in others. Zealous people sometimes make mistakes, but it is far worse to be without zeal.

Conclusion

Let me try now to bring this subject home to every conscience.

1. I have a warning for those who *make no definite profession of Christian faith*. You know nothing of true Christian

zeal. Perhaps you are zealous about your business, or about politics, or about your day-to-day concerns, but you have no zeal for God, for heaven and for eternity. I appeal to you to wake up! You are a fool to be zealous about earthly things, and yet neglect eternal matters.

2. I have something to say to those who do make a definite profession of faith in Christ, and *yet show no Christian zeal*. You must know that there is something seriously wrong with you. I call upon you, in the name of the Lord, to repent. Think of the precious souls who are dying while you sleep. Think of the shortness of time. What you are going to do must be done now or it will not be done at all. Think of the devil, and his zeal to do harm. Think of your Saviour, and all his zeal for you. Think of him in Gethsemane and on Calvary. What are you doing for him? Oh, awake! Be zealous and repent!

3. I have an encouragement for those who *are zealous Christians*. I have only one request - persevere! Do not leave your first love. Do not become cold. Remember that "night comes, when no one can work" (John 9:4). Do not fear the reproach of men. Let them call you whatever they will. Your concern is not with what men think of you now, but with what God will think of you on the Day of Judgment!

8.
HAPPINESS

"Happy are the people whose God is the Lord!" - Psalm 144:15

Happiness is characteristic of those who live in a right relationship with God. Others do not experience true and lasting happiness. I want to consider the subject of happiness under three headings.

1. Things which are essential to happiness

Everyone wants to be happy. That is natural. But how few people really understand what happiness is! I want to show you certain things which are essential to all happiness.

True happiness is not perfect freedom from sorrow and discomfort. In this fallen, sinful world, no such happiness exists anywhere. Nor does true happiness consist in laughter and smiles. Many people laugh loudly and are apparently happy in company, but inwardly they are miserable, and afraid of being alone. Don't be deceived by the emptiness of worldly joviality!

For someone to be truly happy, their deepest needs must be satisfied. The little child is happy when clothed and fed and lying in his mother's arms, because all his needs have been met. It is the same with us all - our deepest needs must be met before we can be truly happy.

What are our deepest needs? Not simply those of the body!

Man has a mind and a conscience. He has an inner sense that this life is not all: there is a life beyond the grave. It is not only his bodily needs that must be satisfied, but the needs of his soul and conscience as well.

If we are to be truly happy, our happiness must not depend on anything in this world. Everything on earth is uncertain and unstable. All that money can buy is temporary. All our relationships will be cut off by death. Lasting happiness cannot depend upon such things.

To be truly happy we must also be able to look all around us without feeling uncomfortable. We must be able to look back to the past without guilty fears. We must be able to look to the future without anxiety. If you cannot look both backwards and forwards without discomfort, you cannot be happy. Your present circumstances may be good, but that is not enough to make you truly happy.

2. Common mistakes about happiness

Many people look for happiness in entirely the wrong places. I want now to warn you plainly against some common mistakes about the way to be happy.

Achievement and success do not bring happiness. Successful men are not necessarily happy. Their very success often brings troubles of its own. *Riches* do not bring happiness. Riches may buy everything except inward peace. *Learning* and *knowledge* do not by themselves bring happiness. Our hearts and consciences need food as well as our minds. Secular knowledge does not give a man happiness when he thinks about death. *A life of ease* does not bring happiness. Often a working man may be tempted to wish he did not have to go to work, and that he could spend his days as he pleased. But God made man to work, and work of some kind is essential for our happiness. *Pleasure* does not bring happiness. Many spend their time in pleasure-seeking, like a child playing with a toy. But even a child does not play with its toy all day long. And men and women have far higher activities in which to engage than the endless pursuit of pleasure.

I want to tell you plainly that if you think any of these things is the way to happiness, you are completely wrong. The whole of human experience is against it. King Solomon had power, wisdom, and wealth far greater than any other man of his day. We know from his own confession that he experimented to see what happiness could be found in these things. Here is his conclusion, written under the inspiration of the Holy Spirit: "All is vanity, and grasping for the wind" (Ecclesiastes 1:14). Countless other testimonies to the same effect can be found throughout history, from men and women who have sought happiness in the wrong places. They achieved their goals in life, but did not find peace and happiness.

Are you a young person? I appeal to you, do not spend your life looking for happiness where it cannot be found. Are you poor? Do you sometimes think that if only you were rich you would be happy? Resist that temptation. There is as much misery among the rich as among the poor. I appeal to you all: remember how common these mistakes about the way to happiness are, and learn to seek it where it is to be found!

3. The way to be happy

Finally, let me show you the way to be truly happy. There is a path which leads to true happiness for all who take it. It is not uncertain or doubtful. True happiness is available to all. But there is only one path, and all who desire to be happy must go the same way.

The only way to be happy is to be a real, earnest, true-hearted Christian. The true Christian is the *only* truly happy man. By a true Christian, I do not mean everybody who calls himself a Christian. I mean the person who has been taught by the Holy Spirit to feel his sins; who has placed all his hope and trust in the Lord Jesus Christ - the person who has been born again and lives a spiritual and holy life.

When I say that that man is truly happy, I do not mean he has no anxieties or troubles of any kind, or that he never sheds tears. But deep down in his heart he has a solid peace and true joy. That is happiness. I do not say that all Christians are equally happy. But compared to the men of the world, all are happy people.

The true Christian has a conscience which is at peace. He knows that Christ has taken away his sins. He alone can think calmly about his soul, for he knows that it is safe in Christ. He alone has sources of happiness which do not depend on this world. However much his earthly circumstances may change, his Friend in heaven remains constant. The true Christian is fulfilling the purpose for which God made him. The unconverted man is not fulfilling it, and cannot be happy.

Without Christ, no man in this world can be truly happy, however great his circumstances. But with Christ, a man can be happy in spite of being poor. He can be happy in spite of being ill. He can be happy in spite of political and social upheavals. His happiness does not depend on his present circumstances. He knows that "it shall be well with the righteous" (Isaiah 3:10).

Objections Answered

As you read, is Satan filling your mind with objections to what I say? If so, I am not afraid to meet them directly.

Perhaps you think you know many religious people who are not happy. But are you sure that these people are true believers in Christ? Many have only an outward form of Christianity, and you must not expect such people to have inward peace and joy.

Perhaps you know some truly spiritual people who do not seem happy. They complain much about their own hearts. They seem to be all doubts, anxieties and fears. I am sorry that there are indeed such Christians, living far below their privileges, and apparently not experiencing this joy and peace. But, have you ever asked them if they would give up their faith and go back to the world? Have you asked them, "Don't you think you would be happier if you stopped following the Lord Jesus?" If you asked these questions, even the weakest and lowest Christians would give you one answer: "Our faith may be weak, and our joy in Christ almost non-existent, but we would never give up what we have!" The root of happiness is there after all, even though neither leaves nor blossom can be seen.

But perhaps you will tell me that you do not think most Christians can be happy because they seem so grave and serious. Have you ever asked yourself why they are serious? Do you expect them to be in your company without a measure of sorrow, when they see you on your way to hell? A learned philosopher once asked a Christian minister why religious people always seemed so sad. The minister replied, "The sight of you, Mr Hume, would make any Christian sad." Only when you yourself are a converted man will you be able to assess truly the gravity of Christians. When you see them in company where all are of one heart, and all love Christ, it is my experience that you will find no one as truly happy as true Christians are.

So then, I repeat my assertion that there is no happiness in the world to compare with that of a true Christian.

Conclusion

In conclusion, let me appeal to the consciences of all my readers.

1. Let me ask you a question. *Are you happy?* If you are living for this world, you know in your heart that you are not truly happy. Let me warn you in love - you will never be happy as long as you turn your back on God and on Christ.

2. Let me give you a warning. *It is a foolish thing to live a life which cannot make you happy.* You are "spending money for what is not bread, and your wages for what does not satisfy"

(Isaiah 55:2). The way of salvation and the way of happiness are the same road! Refuse that way, and you can never be happy.

3. Let me appeal to you to *seek happiness in the only place where it can be found*. It is found in Christ alone. He alone can give it. Come to him, confessing your sin and wretchedness. Come to him, asking him for mercy, for forgiveness, for new life. Do not delay for anything! Come to him now!

4. Let me offer some advice to true Christians as to *how to increase their happiness*.

First, labour to *grow in grace* year by year. Beware of standing still, of living on past experience. Strive to go forward. Read the Bible more earnestly; pray more fervently; hate sin more; deny yourself more; keep your conscience clear of little sins; avoid grieving the Spirit. The holiest men are always the happiest.

Secondly, labour to *be more thankful* year by year. Learn to praise God more for his goodness.

Thirdly, labour to *do more good* year by year. God is good, and does good (Psalm 119:68). Strive to be like God, by doing good. There is something you can do for God. Strive to find it, and do it for him. Remember that the Christian who is compromising and holding back will never enjoy perfect peace. The most committed Christian will always be the happiest man.

9.
FORMALITY

"Having a form of godliness but denying its power." - 2 Timothy 3:5
"He is not a Jew who is one outwardly, nor is that circumcision which is outward in the flesh; but he is a Jew who is one inwardly; and circumcision is that of the heart, in the Spirit, and not in the letter; whose praise is not from men but from God." - Romans 2:28,29

These verses teach us at least three important truths - first, that outward Christianity is not true Christianity; secondly, that true Christianity must live in the heart; and thirdly, that true Christianity must never expect to be popular.

1. Outward Christianity is not true Christianity

The first thing we learn is that outward Christianity is not true Christianity, and an outward Christian is not a true Christian. By an outward Christian I mean someone who is a Christian only in name, and not in reality - in his outward practices but not in his heart.

There are many people whose Christianity consists in nothing more than *attending church*. They do that regularly, but they are not familiar with the Scriptures, and take no delight in reading them. Their lives are not separated from the world. They are not particularly interested in Christian doctrine, and show no concern about what kind of teaching they hear. Such people are only "outward Christians".

There are others whose Christianity consists only in *words*. They know the theory of the Gospel, and hold firmly to sound doctrine. But they know nothing of practical godliness. They are not truthful, loving, humble, honest, kind, gentle, unselfish. They are Christians in name, but they are only "outward Christians".

Scripture speaks very plainly about such outward Christianity. Listen to Paul's words: "He is not a Jew who is one outwardly, nor is that circumcision which is outward in the flesh." These are strong words! A man could be a physical descendant of Abraham, circumcised, a keeper of all the feasts, a regular worshipper in the temple, and yet in God's sight not be a true Jew! In the same way, someone may be a Christian by outward profession, baptised, a regular attender at church, and yet in God's sight not be a Christian at all!

Read Isaiah 1:10-15. There God declares that the sacrifices of the people were useless, and that he hated their feasts. Yet these sacrifices and feasts had been appointed by God himself. God is declaring that even his own ordinances of worship are useless when they are not observed from the *heart*. In fact, they are worse than useless: they are offensive to God, and he hates them.

Listen now to the Lord Jesus Christ himself. He said to the Jews of his day, "These people draw near to me with their mouth, and honour me with their lips, but their heart is far from me, and in vain they worship me" (Matthew 15:8,9). He repeatedly denounced the outward religion of the scribes and Pharisees, warning his disciples against it. Jesus always had a word of kindness for the worst of sinners, and held a door open to them. But he exposed those who had an outward appearance of religion in the severest language.

We could easily point to other places where the Bible speaks about this. The Bible teaches us very plainly that we must not only avoid sin, but also that we must avoid the danger of having nothing but an outward shell of Christianity.

This outward kind of Christianity is very *common*. It invades every kind of Christian church. It is also very *dangerous*. The outward actions of Christianity without the heart have a hardening effect on the heart and conscience. It is also very *foolish*. How foolish to suppose that the outward form of Christianity will bring comfort in a time of illness and at the approach of death! A picture of a fire cannot warm a man, because it is not the real thing. Neither can outward Christianity bring peace to the soul. God sees through it, even if our friends, fellow church members and pastors are deceived by it. God knows the secrets of our *hearts*. He will "judge the secrets of men" at the last day.

2. True Christianity must live in the heart

The heart is the real test both of a man's character and of his religion. It is in the heart that true Christianity must live. Men look at the things a man says and does, but a man may say and do the right things from wrong motives. So God examines the heart. It is there that true, saving Christianity must begin. God says, "I will give you a new heart, and put a new spirit within you" (Ezekiel 36:26). Saving faith is a matter of the heart. "With the heart one believes" (Romans 10:10). Holiness springs from a renewed heart. Christians do the will of God from the heart.

Perhaps some reader thinks that an outwardly correct religion is sufficient. If so, you are completely wrong. The apostle Paul says, "In Christ Jesus neither circumcision not uncircumcision avails anything, but a new creation" (Galatians 6:15). By this he meant much more than simply that circumcision was no longer required under the New Covenant. He meant that true Christianity is not something outward, but something inward. It does not consist in outward ceremonies of any kind, but in God's grace working in our hearts.

When our hearts are wrong, in God's sight everything is wrong. Outward observances are useless if our hearts are wrong. Under the Old Covenant, the Ark was the most sacred thing in the Tabernacle. But when the Israelites trusted in *it* rather than in God, they were beaten by their enemies. They were trusting in an outward object instead of in God himself. Their hearts were wrong. *Our* worship may be outwardly correct, but it will be rejected by God if our hearts are wrong.

When our hearts are right, God will overlook much that is imperfect in us. Jehoshaphat and Asa were kings of Judah who were far from perfect. In many ways they were weak men, yet for all their faults their *hearts* were right. The Passover which Hezekiah kept had many irregularities. But we read that Hezekiah prayed "May the good LORD provide atonement for everyone who *prepares his heart* to seek God" (2 Chronicles 30:18). God answered his prayer. God is far more concerned with the state of our hearts than with outward observance.

Let me exhort you, Resolve to be a Christian in *heart*. You must not neglect the outward aspects of worship, but ensure that above all you are concerned about the state of your heart.

3. True Christianity is never popular

I want you to be a Christian in heart. But I want you to realise that such Christianity will never be popular. It never has been, nor will be, as long as human nature is as the Bible describes it. Most men will be satisfied with an outward religion. It satisfies the conscience that has never seen its need of Christ. It pleases our self-righteousness. It pleases our natural laziness, for heart-Christianity is not easy, whereas outward Christianity need cause us no great trouble.

The history of religion demonstrates what I am saying. In Israel's history, from the start of Exodus to the end of the Acts of the Apostles you will find the same thing. The Old Testament prophets constantly denounced the people for practising outward religion, when their hearts were not in it. The Lord Jesus denounced the Pharisees and scribes for the same thing. After the days of the apostles, how quickly heart-Christianity gave way to something merely outward. This has always been the popular form of Christianity, while true heart-Christianity has been rare.

Heart-Christianity is too *humbling* to be popular. It leaves a man with no room for boasting. It tells him he is dead in sin and must be born of the Spirit. It tells him that he is guilty and hell-deserving and must flee to Christ to be saved. But human pride rebels against being told such things.

Heart-Christianity is also too *holy* to be popular. It requires a man to change his ways. It requires him to forsake the world and his sins, to be spiritually minded, and to love God's Word and prayer. How could such a thing ever be popular? It was never popular in the past, and it is not popular today.

But what does popularity with men matter? We shall not stand before men in the judgment, but before God. And the glory of heart-Christianity is this: it has "the praise of God". God is pleased with what he sees of true heart-Christianity in the present life. Wherever he sees repentance, faith, holiness and the love of God existing in the heart, God is well pleased. Is that not worth more than the praise of men?

On the Day of Judgment, God will proclaim his approval of heart-Christianity before the whole world. He will gather his saints from every part of the world into one glorious company. He will place them at the right hand of Christ's glorious throne. Then, all who have loved and served Christ from their heart will hear him say, "Come, you blessed of my Father, inherit the kingdom prepared for you from the foundation of the world" (Matthew 25:34). Outward Christians will look on with envy, but these words will never be addressed to them. On that great day we shall see and understand fully the true value of heart-Christianity. In this life you are likely to have mockery, unkindness, opposition and persecution. "Through much tribulation we must enter the Kingdom" (Acts 14:22). But whatever you may lose in this world, the praise of God on that day will make up for it all.

Conclusion

Let me close with three plain words of application.

1. Is your Christianity a matter of outward observance rather than of the heart? If so, I must lovingly warn you that you are in the greatest possible danger. You have got nothing to comfort you in a day of trial, nothing to give you hope when you are dying, and nothing to save you at the last day. May God apply this warning to your soul!

2. If your heart condemns you, there is only one course for you to take. You must go to Christ without delay, and tell him your condition. Confess the worthlessness of your outward form of Christianity, and ask him for a new heart. He is mighty to save. No case is too hard for him. "Ask, and it shall be given you; seek, and you shall find; knock, and it shall be opened to you" (Luke 11:9).

3. If your Christianity really is a matter of the heart, and you have a well-grounded confidence towards God, take seriously the responsibilities of your position. Give daily praise and thanks to God, who has given you a new heart. But watch, and be on your guard, in case you lapse into formalism. Watch over your Bible reading, your praying, your daily life and conduct. No one is so spiritual that he cannot have a sad fall. Watch, therefore, and be on your guard, as you look forward to the coming of the Lord. He will soon be here. The time of temptation will soon be over. On that day no one will ever imagine that he gave his heart too thoroughly to Christ.

10.
THE WORLD

"Come out from among them and be separate, says the Lord."
- 2 Corinthians 6:17

Separation from the world is a very important duty. Everyone who professes to be a Christian should consider it very seriously, for separation from the world has always been one of the evidences of God's work of grace in the heart. Those who have really been born of God's Spirit have always separated from the world, whereas those who are Christians only in name always refuse to "come out and be separate". The subject is especially important today, because many are trying to make Christianity as easy as possible and to avoid the need for self-denial. Many think they may behave just as they like and still be good Christians. I want to warn you plainly against this way of thinking.

1. The world is a source of great danger to the soul

By "the world", I do not mean the physical world in which we live. Nothing that God created in the universe is in itself harmful to a man's soul. The whole creation is "very good" (Genesis 1:31). The idea that anything physical is in itself sinful is a foolish error. When I speak of "the world" I mean those people who think only (or mainly) of the things of this world and neglect the world to come - those who think more about the body than the spirit, more about pleasing men than about pleasing God. By "the world" I mean these people, together with their way of life, their opinions, their tastes, their ambitions and their outlook. This is the world which is dangerous to the soul. This is the world from which we must "come out and be separate".

What does God's Word say about this matter? The Apostle Paul says, "Do not be conformed to this world" (Romans 12:2). Look up also 1 Corinthians 2:12, Galatians 1:4, Ephesians 2:2, and 2 Timothy 4:10. James says, "Do you not know that friendship with the world is enmity with God? Whoever therefore wants to be a friend of the world makes himself an enemy of God" (James 4:4). See also James 1:27. The Apostle John says, "Do not love the world or the things in the world. If anyone loves the world, the love of the Father is not in him" (1 John 2:15). Look up also 1 John 2:16-17, 3:1, 4:5, 5:4, and 5:19. And the Lord Jesus himself, speaking about his disciples says, "They are not of the world, just as I am not of the world" (John 17:16). Look up also Matthew 13:22, John 8:23, 14:17, 15:18,19 and 16:33.

These texts speak for themselves. No rational person can deny that they teach that "the world" is the Christian's enemy, and that friendship of the world and friendship of Christ are completely opposed to each other.

Moreover, Christian experience confirms this. The greatest cause of damage to Christ's cause is love of the world. Thousands who think they are Christians get shipwrecked here. They do not deliberately choose evil, or reject any biblical doctrine. But they love the world and must keep in with it. It is their love of the world which leads them down the broad way to destruction.

2. Wrong ideas about separation from the world

Let me now show you what separation from the world does *not* mean. It is important to be clear about this, for sometimes Christians can do great harm by acting on a false understanding of what separation from the world means.

When God says, "Come out and be separate", this does *not* mean that *Christians should give up their work in the world.* Cornelius the soldier, Luke the doctor and Zenas the lawyer are examples of men in secular work. In fact, it is sinful to be idle, and idleness often leads us into temptation. So it is right that we should have a lawful job of work. We must not give up any occupation (unless it is sinful in and of itself) out of fear that it will harm us. That is lazy and cowardly conduct. What we ought to do is to take our Christianity with us into our places of employment in the world.

It does *not* mean that *Christians should have nothing at all to do with unconverted people.* Our Lord and his disciples went to a marriage feast. They had a meal in a Pharisee's house. In 1 Corinthians 10:27 the apostle Paul tells us how to behave if an unbeliever invites us to a feast; he does not tell us not to go. We must not cut ourselves off in this way from opportunities of doing good. If Christ is with us wherever we go, we may be the means of saving others without harming ourselves.

It does *not* mean that *Christians should take no interest in anything except religion.* Some may think it very spiritual to neglect science, art, literature, and politics, to read no books except spiritual ones, to read no newspapers and to know nothing about the government of their country. I think that is an idle and selfish neglect of duty. Paul valued good government (1 Timothy 2:2); he quoted heathen writers in his sermons; he knew the laws and customs of the world, as we see from his illustrations. Christians who pride themselves on ignorance bring religion into contempt.

It does *not* mean that *Christians should be eccentric in their dress, manners or voice.* We should never attract attention to ourselves by these means. There is no reason to suppose that our Lord and his disciples dressed and behaved differently from others of their own society. The Lord condemned the Pharisees for "making broad their phylacteries and enlarging the borders of their garments" so as to be "seen by men".

It does *not* mean that *Christians should retire from society and live in solitude*. Our Lord prayed distinctly, "I do not pray that you should take them out of the world, but that you should keep them from the evil one" (John 17:15). We cannot keep the devil out of our hearts by retreating into a corner. True Christianity and unworldliness are better seen when we manfully stand our ground and show the power of grace to overcome evil, than when we forsake the post where God has placed us.

It does *not* mean that *Christians ought to withdraw from every church which is imperfect*. In all Paul's letters we see the faults and corruptions of churches reproved, but Christians are never told to leave those churches because they were not perfect.

I ask you to consider these six points carefully. I have seen many people make mistakes in relation to each of them, and much misery and unhappiness caused by those mistakes. I want to put you on your guard against them. Avoid rushing into courses of action which you will afterwards regret. Let me give you (especially if you are a young Christian) two pieces of advice:

First, remember that the shortest path is not always the path of duty. You may think it right to quarrel with all your unconverted relatives, cut off all your friends, withdraw completely from society, give up every act of normal courtesy and devote yourself entirely to the direct work of Christ. It may satisfy your conscience and save you trouble. But often it is a selfish, lazy, self-pleasing way to behave. Often the true way of bearing our cross is to deny ourselves and adopt a very different course of action.

Secondly, if you want to come out from the world, beware of a sour, unattractive, gloomy and unpleasant way of behaving. Never forget that there is such a thing as "winning without the word" (1 Peter 3:1). Strive to show others that your principles (whatever they may think about them) make you cheerful, agreeable, good-tempered, unselfish, considerate of others and ready to take an interest in everything that is innocent and good. Let there be no *needless* separation. In many things we *must* be separate. But be careful that it is the right kind of separation. If the world is offended by the separation that the Bible requires, we cannot help that, but let us make sure we do not offend by a separation that is foolish and unscriptural.

3. What separation from the world really means

Let me now show you *what true separation from the world really means*. I shall try to lay down general principles, which you must apply in detail for yourself.

1. You must consistently *refuse to be guided by the world's standard of right and wrong*. Don't do things just because "everybody does them". Your standard must be the Word of God alone.

2. You must *be very careful how you spend your leisure time*. This is very important, for often our leisure time is a time of temptation. Be careful how you spend your evenings, and make sure that you always make time for quiet thought, Bible reading and prayer.

3. You must *consistently resolve not to be swallowed up and absorbed by the business of the world*. As a Christian you must strive to do your earthly business to the very best of your ability. But you must not allow it to come between you and Christ. If your earthly business begins to encroach upon your Sundays, and to crowd out Bible reading and prayer, then it is taking over your life. Like Daniel, you must be prepared to make time for communion with God, no matter what the cost involved (Daniel 6:10).

4. You must *abstain from all entertainments which are inseparably connected with sin*. This is a difficult subject, but one we need to consider. The fact is that some entertainments may be innocent when considered in and of themselves. But we must also consider whether *in practice* they are inseparably

accompanied by sin. If so, we must abstain from them.

5. You must *be moderate in your use of lawful and innocent recreations*. We all need recreation, both for our bodies and for our minds. But even good and right recreations become wrong when they take up too much of our time and attention. We may use them in order to strengthen mind and body so that we may serve Christ better. But if they begin to interfere with our serving Christ, we must exercise restraint.

6. You must *be careful about friendships and close relationships with worldly people*. I am not saying you should have nothing to do with unconverted people. In everyday life we must have dealings with them, and must always treat them with the utmost courtesy, kindness and love. But intimate friendship is quite a different matter. If you choose for your close friends people who care nothing about salvation, or Christ, or the Bible, I cannot see how you can hope to progress as a Christian. The consistent Christian will soon find that his tastes and ways are not the same as theirs, and will have to choose between the two. And it is particularly important to realise this when it comes to choosing a husband or wife. A consistent Christian cannot possibly choose a worldly partner without doing immense harm to his spiritual life or happiness. If you are not yet married, make it your resolve that you will not even consider marrying someone who is not a decided Christian.

I ask you to give serious thought to these six principles. But what should you do when you are uncertain how to apply them in a particular situation? First, you should pray for wisdom. Ask God to give you sound judgment. Then, remember that God's eye is always upon you. That will help you make the right choice. Ask yourself which course of action you would want to be found pursuing when Christ comes again. Also, it is right to consider how other holy Christians have behaved in similar circumstances. If we cannot see clearly our own way, it is not wrong to follow good examples.

4. The secret of victory over the world

Let me now show you *the secret of victory over the world*.

The first secret is *a right heart*. A man's desires and tastes will only be spiritual when his heart has been renewed by the Holy Spirit, and Christ dwells there. If you want to be separate from the world, make sure you have a new heart!

The second secret is *a lively practical faith in unseen things*. Scripture says, "This is the victory that has overcome the world — our faith" (1 John 5:4). The more we realise the reality of spiritual things - of God, Christ, heaven, hell, judgment, eternity - the more we shall be able to leave the things of the world.

The third secret is *the habit of confessing Christ boldly whenever it is appropriate*. We must not be ashamed of Christ. Quietly and politely we must let men see that we act upon Christian principles and that we do not intend to swerve from them. At first this will be hard, but it will make life much easier eventually. When people clearly understand that we serve Christ, they will expect us to live differently, and that will make it easier for us to do so.

Conclusion

Let me finish with some words of application.

1. Are you overcoming the world, or are you being overcome by it? Are you separated from the world, or are you not? The question is important, for the world is passing away, and those who cling to the world will perish with it. I appeal to you to wake up and flee from the wrath to come.

2. If you want to come out from the world, but do not know where to begin, you should go directly, as a sinner, to the Lord Jesus Christ and put the whole matter in his hands. Christ "gave himself for our sins, that he might deliver us from this present evil world" (Galatians 1:4). He is "able to save to the uttermost

those who come to God through him" (Hebrews 7:25). It may seem hard to come out of the world and be separate, but you will find that with Jesus nothing is impossible. You - yes, you - will be able to overcome the world!

3. If you have come out of the world, take comfort and persevere. You are on the right road. Continue on it. Do not be ashamed of standing alone. Remember that the most decided Christians are always the happiest eventually. Never be ashamed of coming out of the world and being separate.

11.
WEALTH AND POVERTY

"There was a certain rich man who was clothed in purple and fine linen and fared sumptuously every day. But there was a certain beggar named Lazarus, full of sores, who was laid at his gate, desiring to be fed with the crumbs which fell from the rich man's table. Moreover the dogs came and licked his sores. So it was that the beggar died, and was carried by the angels to Abraham's bosom. The rich man also died and was buried. And being in torments in Hades, he lifted up his eyes and saw Abraham afar off, and Lazarus in his bosom." - Luke 16:19-23

Most Bible readers will be familiar with the parable of the rich man and Lazarus. It is unforgettable. The picture is painted so vividly we could almost imagine we were present and saw it all. But it is one thing to admire the story, and another to learn its spiritual lessons. Thousands know every word of this parable, yet never think of how it applies to them. I ask you to consider the most important truths this parable teaches. I shall consider only the part quoted above. May the Holy Spirit impress these truths upon our souls!

1. God allots very different conditions to different men

What a contrast there is between the two men in the parable! The Lord Jesus speaks of a rich man and a beggar. One has much of this world's goods; the other has nothing. Both are children of Adam; both belong to the human family; both live in the same land under the same government. Yet how different are their conditions!

We must be careful not to read into the parable lessons it was never meant to teach. The rich are not always bad men, and do not always go to hell. And the poor are not always good men, and do not always go to heaven. It is not sinful to be rich, or to be poor. The Lord Jesus does not praise or condemn the condition of either man. He is simply describing things as they often are in the world, and as we must expect them to be.

It is very popular to teach that all men ought to be equal, but as long as the world is in its present state, that can never be. As long as some are wise and some foolish, some strong and some weak, some healthy and some sick, some hard-working and some lazy, together with many other factors, there will always be some rich and some poor. Until sin is cast out of the world, and men's hearts made new and holy, there can never be universal happiness or equality. No government, or education, or politics can bring it about.

This does not mean we should not try to help the poor or to change things. But we must understand that until the Lord Jesus comes again there will always be both rich and poor in the world.

2. A man's worldly position is no test of his spiritual condition

Many would consider the position of the rich man to be ideal. He seems to have had all that his heart could wish. But the truth is that this rich man was desperately poor. When the good things of this life were taken away, he had nothing to take with him for the next life. He had riches on earth, but no treasure in heaven. He had fine clothes, but no covering of righteousness. He had friends on earth, but no Friend and Advocate at God's right hand. He never tasted the bread of life, and when he left his splendid house he had no home to go to in heaven. His "wealth" was not real wealth, for he was without Christ, without faith, without forgiveness and without holiness. When he died he went to hell. In truth, he was desperately poor.

On the other hand, Lazarus had literally nothing in this world. It is hard to imagine a case of greater poverty and misery. But in the highest sense, Lazarus was rich. He was a child of God, with an inheritance in heaven. His riches were lasting and true. He had the very best clothing - the righteousness of Christ. He had the best of friends - God himself. As for food, he fed upon the bread of life. And these things he had for ever - in his death as well as in his life. Lazarus was not poor, but truly rich.

You see then that we must measure men by God's standards, not by the standards of this world. A converted beggar is more honourable in God's eyes than an unconverted President or Prime Minister. A man may be great and admired for a time, but then experience darkness and misery for ever. Another may be despised in this world, yet spend eternity in glory with Christ. Riches and worldly greatness are by no means proofs of God's favour. Often they are a snare and hindrance to a man's soul, making him love the world and forget God. And poverty and trials are not proofs of God's anger. Often they are blessings in disguise, sent in love and wisdom to wean a man from the world and teach him to set his heart on things above. They are sent to show the sinner his own heart and to make God's people fruitful in good works.

One of the great secrets of happiness in this life is to have a contented spirit. Seek daily to realise that this life is not the place of reward. When the day of judgment comes all will be put right. Only then will it be made evident what a great difference there is between those who serve God and those who do not.

3. The rich and the poor alike come to the grave

Though they are so different in their lives, both Lazarus and the rich man meet the same end. They both die. This is the fate of all men, and will be yours too unless the Lord Jesus should return first in glory. Death is the great enemy that no one can conquer. It spares no one, and respects no one. It will not wait until you are ready. It will come in God's appointed hour.

All men know these things, but most do not feel them as realities. If they did, they would act upon them. O how foolish it is to set our hearts on this dying world and its short-lived comforts, and to lose eternal life!

4. A believer's soul is very precious in the sight of God

How precious a believer's soul is in the sight of God! The rich man died and was buried. Probably he had a splendid funeral, but the next thing we read is that he was in torment. Lazarus certainly had no splendid funeral, but he was carried by the angels to a place of rest in Abraham's bosom. This part of the parable helps us to understand the relation between believers and God their Father. It shows a little of the care which the King of kings gives to the least and lowest of Christ's disciples.

No one has friends and attendants like the believer. Angels rejoice when he is born again, protect him in the world, take charge of his soul in death and carry him safely home. Though he may see himself as vile and lowly, yet the lowest and poorest believer is cared for by his Father in heaven, with a care too great to understand. The LORD has become his Shepherd, so that he can lack nothing (Psalm 23:1).

Whenever a man comes sincerely to Christ, he has all the benefits of a sure and certain covenant. All his sins are forgiven and his heart renewed. Christ will bear with him in his ignorance and teach him the truth. Christ will be with him at all times. Nothing can hurt him without God's permission. Whoever persecutes him persecutes Christ himself (Acts 26:15). All his trials are wisely controlled; all things are working together for his good. And when his work is done, the angels of God will come and carry him safely home to glory.

Christian reader, you do not know the full extent of your

privileges and possessions. Learn to live by faith more. Get to know the great treasure waiting for you in Christ even now.

5. Selfishness is a dangerous and soul-ruining sin

I want you to notice, lastly, what a dangerous and soul-ruining sin selfishness is. There was nothing obviously sinful about the outward life of this rich man. He was not a murderer, a thief, an adulterer or a liar. Yet he went to a place of torment. Surely there are lessons we must learn from this.

1. We must beware of *living only for ourselves*. It is not enough to be able to say, "I live correctly; I do my duty in every area of life." The question is, Are you living for yourself or for Christ? What is your purpose and motivation in life? Do you live no longer for yourself but for him who died for you? (See 2 Corinthians 5:15.) If you are like the rich man, living for yourself, you will be lost.

2. We must learn the danger of *not doing what we ought*. The rich man was not in torment because of what he did, but because of what he did not do. He simply left Lazarus at his gate. At the judgment Christ will say to many: "I was hungry and you gave me no food; I was thirsty and you gave me no drink; I was a stranger and you did not take me in ..." (Matthew 25:42,43).

3. We must learn that *riches bring special dangers with them*. Many spend their lives seeking riches, yet riches bring great spiritual danger. They tend to harden the soul, to close the eyes to the things of faith and help us forget God. Jesus says: "How hard it is for those who have riches to enter the kingdom of God!" (Mark 10:23)

We need to learn to be especially careful about selfishness in these last days. "In the last days, perilous times will come: for men will be lovers of themselves, lovers of money" (2 Timothy 3:1,2). Many rich people give away nothing at all, or very little in proportion to their wealth. But the Bible has much to say against selfishness and the love of money. Read the parable which Jesus told about the rich fool who had much wealth but "was not rich towards God" in Luke 12:16-21.

Do you have money? Then "Take heed and beware of covetousness" (Luke 12:15). Certainly it is possible for you to be saved, for Abraham, Job and David were all rich men. But think about your danger. Remember that money is a good servant, but a bad master.

Have you little or no money? Do not envy people who are richer than you. Pity them, pray for them, and do not be quick to judge them. Maybe you would do no better. And remember that it is the love of money that is a root of every kind of evil, and you can love money even without having any. Beware of thinking that being poor will save you. Lazarus did not go to heaven because he was poor, but because he had Christ.

Do you want to know the cure for selfishness? Nothing but a real knowledge of Christ's love will cure it. You must know your own sinful condition, experience the power of Christ's blood to heal you, taste peace with God through Christ and feel the love of God in your heart. Then, knowing how much you owe to Christ, you will feel that nothing is too great to give to him. Selfishness may be concealed by a good nature, love of praise, or wrong ideas about self-denial. But only the love of Christ will actually change it and lead you to live and work for Christ.

Conclusion

Let me conclude with three words of application.

1. I *urge* you to examine yourself. What are you doing? Where are you going? What will be your condition after death? These are solemn questions. I pray that the Holy Spirit will lead many to ask them!

2. I *invite* all who need to be saved to go to Jesus Christ in earnest prayer at once. Seek the Lord while he may be found (Isaiah 55:6). He receives sinners (Luke 15:2). But one day it will be too late, as the Rich Man discovered.

3. I *appeal* to Christians to give generously to all causes of charity and mercy. You cannot keep your money for ever, and one day you must give an account of what you have done with it. I do not mean that we should give away everything, or neglect our work or family. We should work hard and provide for our dependants. We should always be thinking of how we can do most good with our money in our short lives. Could we not spend less on ourselves and more on others? Remember that spiritually we were like Lazarus. We lay sick, helpless and starving at heaven's gate till Jesus came to relieve us. He went about doing good, and died on the cross to save us. Let us be like him in doing good to others.

12.
THE BEST FRIEND

"This is my friend." - Song of Solomon 5:16

A friend is one of the greatest blessings on earth, yet real friends are rare. Many will befriend you in times of prosperity, but a friend who will stay with you when you are sick, helpless and poor is very rare. Above all, there are few friends who will care for your soul. But I want to recommend a real friend to you. He is "a friend who sticks closer than a brother" (Proverbs 18:24). He is ready to be your friend in time and in eternity. The friend I want you to know is the Lord Jesus Christ. You will be a truly happy person if he is your chief friend!

1. The Lord Jesus is a friend of those in need

Because we are sinners, we are in the greatest possible need. By nature we are all sick with a deadly disease. We are all dying through sin. But Christ came to deliver us from this death. By nature we are all great debtors. We owe to God a debt which we can never pay. But Christ came to pay our debt. By nature we were all shipwrecked and cast away. We could never reach the safe harbour of eternal life. But the Lord Jesus came to save that which was lost, and to bring us safely to heaven.

You see, there was no possible way for us to be saved except by Christ's coming into the world to save sinners (1 Timothy 1:15). He was under no obligation to do so, but his own free love, mercy and pity brought him to deliver us. This is true friendship! There has never been a friend like Jesus Christ!

2. The Lord Jesus is an active friend

A true friend is known by his actions rather than by his words. No one's actions ever demonstrated true friendship more than Christ's. Although by nature he was God, for our sakes he took a human nature and became man. For us, he lived for thirty-three years in this evil world, despised and rejected by men, a man of sorrows and acquainted with grief. For us he submitted to the terrible death on the cross. He died for us.

Jesus did not have to do any of these things. But he knew that nothing else could save us, and such was his love that he was prepared to come and die for us. This is friendship beyond our ability to understand. Who can find someone willing to die for those who hate him? Yet this is exactly what Jesus did. There has never been a friend like him!

3. The Lord Jesus is a powerful friend

Often our friends would be willing to help us if only they could. They can sympathise with us when we are in trouble, but they have no power to deliver us from it. But Christ is almighty. He is never in the position of wishing he could help but not having the power to do so.

He is able to forgive even the greatest sinners. Whatever we may have been or done, his blood can cleanse us from all sin. He is able to convert even the hardest heart, and to create a new spirit in a man. He is able to preserve to the end all who believe in him. He can give them grace to overcome the world, the flesh and the devil, and to persevere to the end. He is able to give the best of gifts to those who love him. In this life he can give peace, joy, hope and inward comforts which no money can buy, and after death a crown of glory which never fades. This is true power! No one ever had a powerful friend like Jesus!

4. The Lord Jesus is a loving friend

His love is called "love that passes knowledge" (Ephesians 3:19). He shows his love by his willingness to receive sinners. He turns no one away, however great his sins. He is ready to forgive and to cleanse all who come to him. He shows his love by the way in which he deals with sinners after they have believed in him and become his friends. He is always patient with them, always ready to hear their complaints, always ready to sympathise with all their sorrows. He never allows them to be tempted beyond their ability to endure. He accepts their service, poor as it is. He has caused it to be written in the Bible that he takes pleasure in his people (Psalm 147:11).

The love of the Lord Jesus is not a response to anything lovable in us, but flows from his pure, unselfish compassion. There is no love on earth to compare with it!

5. The Lord Jesus is a wise friend

Not all our friends are wise. They can give bad and harmful advice, even when they mean well. Some friends hold us back from the Christian pathway, and entangle us in the emptiness of the world. But the friendship of the Lord Jesus always does us good, and never harm.

The Lord Jesus never spoils his friends by giving them what they want rather than what is good for them. He gives them everything that really is good for them, but he also requires them to suffer hardship and to bear their cross. Even though they may not like it at the time, he knows that it is for their good, and that they will recognise this when they are brought to heaven. The Lord Jesus never makes mistakes in dealing with his friends.

When we look about us, we see how much harm people so often get from their friends. Friends often encourage one another in worldliness and foolishness rather than in love and good works. Often when they meet together it does them more harm than good. But how different is the friendship of the Lord Jesus, the Friend of sinners! Consider how he treated his disciples, comforting, rebuking and exhorting them with perfect wisdom. Consider the perfect timing of his visit to Mary and Martha at Bethany (John 11). Consider his wise and gracious dealings with Peter on the shore of Galilee (John 21). His company made his friends more holy. His gifts are always for our spiritual good. His kindness is always exercised in wisdom. There never was such a wise friend as Jesus Christ!

6. The Lord Jesus is a proven friend

He has shown friendship to all kinds of people in all sorts of conditions throughout history. Some of his friends have been kings and rich men, like David and Solomon; others have been poor, like the shepherds at Bethlehem. Some have been masters, like Abraham; others have been slaves, like the Christians in Nero's household. Some became his friends in early childhood, like Samuel and Timothy; others did not know him till they were quite old, like Manasseh. Some have been outgoing people like Peter, or full of activity like Martha; others have been quiet like Mary. The Lord Jesus' friends have been taken from every nation of the world. And all of them have found his friendship good. No other friend was ever so fully tried and proved as the Lord Jesus Christ!

7. The Lord Jesus is an unfailing friend

While everything else on earth changes, the friendship of the Lord Jesus never changes. Even husbands sometimes desert their wives, and even parents sometimes abandon their children. But Christ has never abandoned even one of his friends, or changed his feelings towards them. He is "the same, yesterday, today and for ever". There is never any parting between him and his people. When he has made his home in the heart of any sinner, he never leaves it. He says, "I will never leave you nor forsake you" (Hebrews 13:5).

Conclusion

Let me finish with some words of application. I do not know the state of your soul, but I do know that what I have to say is worthy of your attention. I plead with you to give attention now to the Lord Jesus Christ and your own spiritual condition.

1. First, I ask you to *consider very seriously whether Christ is your Friend, and you are a friend of Christ*. I am grieved to say that thousands upon thousands who call themselves Christians are not Christ's friends at all. They are outwardly Christians, but they are not friends of the Lord Jesus. They do not hate the sins which he died to put away. They do not love the Saviour who came into the world to save sinners. They do not delight in the gospel of reconciliation. They do not speak with the Friend of sinners in prayer, or seek close fellowship with him. Such people are not Christ's friends. I appeal to you to examine yourself. Are you or are you not one of Christ's friends?

2. Secondly, I want you to know that *if you are not one of Christ's friends, you are a poor and miserable being*. You are in a world which is passing away, and a world of sorrow, yet you have no real source of comfort or refuge in time of need. You must one day die, but you are not ready to die. Your sins are not forgiven. You are going to be judged, but you are not prepared to meet God. You could be, but you refuse the one Mediator and Advocate who can save you. You love the world more than Christ. You refuse the Friend of sinners. I say again that you are a poor and miserable being.

3. Thirdly, I want you to know that *if you really want a friend, Christ is willing to become your Friend*. He is calling you now through the words which I write. He is ready to receive you, however unworthy you feel, and to number you among his friends. He is ready to forgive all your past, to clothe

you with his righteousness, to give you his Spirit and to make you his own child. All he asks is that you come to him. He tells you to come with all your sins, acknowledging your vileness and confessing your shame. Come just as you are, not waiting for anything. You are unworthy of anything, but he bids you to come and be his friend. Will you not come?

4. Lastly, I want you to know that *if Christ is your Friend, you have great privileges, and ought to live in a way worthy of them.* Every day, seek to have closer communion with him, and to know more of his grace and power. True Christianity is not simply believing a set of abstract truths. It involves living in daily personal communion with a Person. The Apostle Paul said, "To me, to live is Christ" (Philippians 1:21). Seek daily to glorify Christ in everything. "A man who has friends must himself be friendly" (Proverbs 18:24) and no one is under a greater obligation than someone who is a friend of Christ. Avoid everything which would grieve him. Fight hard against besetting sins, inconsistency, slowness to confess him before men. When you are tempted, say to your soul, "Is this your loyalty to your friend?"

Above all, think of the mercy which he has shown to you, and learn to rejoice every day in your Friend! You may be sick; your troubles may be very great; your earthly friends may forsake you and you may be alone in the world. But if you are in Christ you have a Friend - a Friend who is powerful, loving, wise, unfailing. Think much about your Friend!

Soon, your Friend will come and take you home, and you will live with him for ever. At that time the whole world will acknowledge that the truly rich and happy man is the man who has had the Lord Jesus Christ as his Friend.

13.
ILLNESS

"He whom you love is sick." - John 11:3

This brief message, "He whom you love is sick", was sent to the Lord Jesus by Martha and Mary. It was their brother Lazarus who was ill. Lazarus was a Christian, very much loved by the Lord Jesus, yet he was ill. So we must not think that illness is a sign of God's anger. It is intended rather for our good - "All things work together for good to those who love God, to those who are the called according to his purpose" (Romans 8:28).

It is important to consider this subject of illness. You will probably be ill at some time, and to think seriously about the subject in advance may do you much good. We shall consider the subject under three headings.

1. Illness exists everywhere

Illness exists in every part of the world, and among all classes of men. Neither earthly riches nor faith in Christ exempts us from being ill. Illness is often a very humbling experience. It can make a strong man like a little child, and make a courageous man tremble at the least little thing. It can affect our mind and thinking. And it is not preventable by anything that man can do. The average life-expectancy can be increased by medical science. New cures can be found for various diseases. But still "The days of our lives are seventy years; and if by reason of strength they are eighty years, yet their boast is only labour and sorrow, for it is soon cut off, and we fly away" (Psalm 90:10). That was true when Moses wrote it, and it is still true today.

What is the explanation for the universality of illness? Why do people become ill and die? We cannot suppose for a moment that God created illness and disease at the beginning. Everything he created was "very good", and it obviously did not include illness. But the Bible tells us that something has subsequently come into the world which was not there at first. That something is *sin*. And sin is the cause of all the illness, pain and suffering in the world. Without sin there would be no illness.

You see, it is only the Bible that gives us a satisfactory explanation for the facts as they are. The Bible explains how we come to have such marvellously formed bodies. God created them! And the Bible explains how - despite being created by a God who is infinitely wise and good - we are now prone to illness and suffering. The great biblical doctrines of creation and the Fall are the only explanation.

2. Illness can do good to men

Perhaps you find it surprising to learn that illness can do us good. Many people never consider that. They look only on the suffering and pain, and see no good in it at all. Now I agree that if there were no sin in the world, it would be impossible for illness to do men good. There was no illness in the sinless world which God created. But God has wisely permitted it since the Fall of man, and I see it as just as much a blessing as a curse. God is able to use our temporary pain and suffering for the higher good of our heart, mind, conscience and soul to all eternity.

Illness helps *to remind men of death*. Most men live as though they were never going to die, and make no preparation.

Illness can remind them about what they would otherwise prefer to forget.

Illness helps *to make us think seriously about God*. Many people while they are healthy choose to forget about God and their relationship with him. Illness can remind them that they must one day meet God.

Illness helps *to change our outlook on life*. Many people never think about anything except their happiness in this world. A long period of illness can change their assessment of things they thought so important before. For example, the man who loves money may learn that his money cannot comfort him when he is ill.

Illness helps *to humble us*. We are all proud by nature. We find somebody to look down on. But illness shows us our weakness. It comes to the rich and the poor, the famous and the unknown, and it puts us all on the same level.

Illness helps *to test our Christianity*. It helps us to learn whether our Christianity is real - whether it is built on a solid foundation. Many people are not building on a solid foundation, and a time of illness may reveal to them that their "Christianity" brings them no comfort in a time of trial.

I do not want you to think that illness always benefits people in these ways. By no means! Many experience illness, and learn nothing from it at all, as their subsequent behaviour shows. Their hearts are hard, and it does them no good.

But there are many people to whom God has made illness a blessing. God has used it to speak to them, and to lead them to seek Christ. So we should never complain about illness. If we respond to it properly, it may do us great good.

3. Illness calls us to special duties

I want to be practical and specific about the special duties to which illness calls us. I want you to be quite clear about what you ought to do in this world of disease and death.

The first duty of which illness reminds us is *to live in such a way that we are always ready to meet God*. Illness reminds us of death, the door through which we must pass to judgment. In that judgment we shall see God face to face. So the first lesson illness should teach us is to prepare to meet God.

When will you be prepared to meet God? Only when your sins are forgiven, your heart is renewed and your will is taught to delight in the will of God. You have many sins, and only the blood of Jesus Christ can wash those sins away. Only his righteousness can make you acceptable in God's presence. And these benefits are received by faith alone. So if you want to know whether you are ready to meet God, you must ask, "Do I have faith?" By nature your heart is unfit for God's company. Only the Holy Spirit can transform you, make all things new and give you a delight in doing God's will. So if you want to know whether you are ready to meet God, ask yourself another question: "Have my heart and life been changed by the Holy Spirit?"

Nothing less than this will prepare us to meet God. We must be justified, and we must be sanctified. Christ's blood must sprinkle us, and Christ's Spirit must live in us. These are the essentials of the Christian faith, and in this world of illness and death your first duty is to make sure you possess these things.

A second duty of which illness reminds us is *always to live in such a way as to be able to bear it patiently*. It is not an easy thing to be ill. We may be cut off from our usual activities; our plans may be disrupted; we may have to endure long hours of weariness and pain. All this may be a great strain upon us, and greatly try our patience. So we ought to learn patience while we are healthy, before any of these things happen to us. We should pray that the Holy Spirit will sanctify our temper and outlook. We must make real work of prayer, asking regularly for strength to bear God's will as well as for strength to do God's will. Remember that the needed strength is there to be had. "If you ask anything in my name, I will do it" (John 14:14).

I want to emphasise this point. I believe that the passive graces of Christianity do not receive the attention which they ought. Meekness, gentleness, long-suffering, faith and patience are all fruits of the Spirit. They glorify God. Often men who despise the active side of a Christian's life are compelled to think seriously when they see these passive graces in his life. And it is during a time of illness that these graces are often most clearly seen. Many Christians have had a lasting influence upon others, not by their words, but by the way in which they have responded to illness.

Do you want to make your Christianity attractive and beautiful to others? Then acquire the grace of patience now, before you experience illness. Then, if you become ill, your illness will be for the glory of God.

A third duty of which illness reminds us is *always to be ready to sympathise with and help our fellow men*. There is always someone near you who is ill, perhaps in your family, or in your church or neighbourhood. You should see this as an opportunity to do good. It may need only a friendly enquiry, or an expression of concern, or perhaps a sympathetic visit. Such simple acts of kindness have a tendency to remove barriers and create good feeling. They may be the means of ultimately leading men to Christ. They are the kind of good works for which every Christian should be ready. In this world of illness and disease we ought to "bear one another's burdens" (Galatians 6:2) and "be kind one to another" (Ephesians 4:32). Conscientious attention to such acts of kindness is one of the clearest evidences of having "the mind of Christ". The Lord Jesus himself "went about doing good" to those who were ill and suffering (Acts 10:38). The importance which he attaches to such acts is shown in his description of his own people at the last judgment, where he says, "I was ill, and you visited me" (Matthew 25:36).

Do you want to prove the reality of your Christian love? If so, then beware of a selfish neglect of your sick brothers and sisters. Watch out for them. Give them the help they need. Sympathise with them, and try to lighten their burden. Above all, strive to do them spiritual good. It will do *you* good even if it does not benefit them. I firmly believe that God is testing and proving us by every case of illness within our reach. By permitting suffering, God tests whether Christians have any feeling. Beware lest you be tested and found lacking! If you can live in a sick and dying world and not feel for others, you still have much to learn.

Conclusion

Let me now finish with four words of practical application.

1. First, I ask a question. What will *you* do when you are ill? For everyone, the time comes for illness and death. Sooner or later that time must come for you. What will you do? Where will you turn for comfort? On what do you mean to build your hope? I plead with you not to put these questions away. Let them work on your conscience, and give yourself no rest till you can answer them satisfactorily. Your eternal destiny is far too important for you to put these questions off. The most important business of life ought not to be left till last. You cannot presume you will be able to repent on your death-bed. Two criminals were crucified with Jesus. One repented at the end. The other did not. You have no reason to suppose that you will be able to repent on your deathbed if you will not repent now.

If you were going to live for ever in this world, I would not address you like this. But you are not going to live here for ever. You are going to die, and I want you to be ready for that day. Think, I plead with you, what an awful thing it will be if you have made provision for everything except the one thing which is truly necessary.

2. Secondly, I offer advice to all who need it and are willing to receive it. I offer it to all who are not ready to meet God. Get to know the Lord Jesus Christ without delay. Repent, be converted, flee to Christ and be saved. No gambler on earth is as foolish as the man who gambles with his soul - the man who is unprepared to meet God and yet puts off repentance. You

know that your sins need to be dealt with. You know that you need a Saviour. Then go to him today, and cry to him to save your soul. Go at once. Seek him by faith. Commit your soul to him. Ask him for pardon and peace with God. Ask him to pour out the Holy Spirit on you and make you a true Christian. He will hear you. Whatever you may have been, he will not refuse your prayer. He has said, "The one who comes to me I will by no means cast out" (John 6:37).

I plead with you to beware of a vague, indefinite Christianity. Do not think that all will be well because you are a church member. Nothing but a personal relationship with Christ himself will do. Do not rest, I plead with you, till you have the testimony of the Holy Spirit himself in your heart that you have been washed, and sanctified, and justified, and made one with Christ. Vague, indefinite religion may seem quite adequate when you are healthy. But it will never do when you are ill. It will break down completely when the end is in sight. Only Christ can rob death of its sting, and enable us to face our last illness without fear. We need to be united to him. We need to know and believe in him as our Priest who intercedes for us at God's right hand. He alone can deliver those who through fear of death are in bondage. If you desire to have hope and comfort in your illness, get to know Christ. Seek him now.

3. Thirdly, I exhort all true Christians to remember how much they may glorify God in time of illness, and to lie quiet in God's hand when they are ill. This is a very important matter. I know how ready the heart of the believer is to faint. I know how busy Satan is in suggesting doubts and questionings when the believer's body is weak. I have seen something of the depression which can come upon God's children when they are suddenly ill and compelled to rest.

I earnestly ask all sick believers to remember that they may honour God as much by patient suffering as by active work. It often demonstrates more grace to rest quietly than to be hard at work. I appeal to them to remember that Christ cares for them as much when they are ill as when they are well. The

100

chastening which they experience is sent in love, and not in anger. Remember above all Jesus' sympathy for his weak members. They are always cared for tenderly, but especially in their time of need. Christ has much experience of illness. He knows the heart of a sick man. Very often illness and suffering make believers more like their Lord. "He himself took our infirmities and bore our illnesses" (Matthew 8:17). The Lord Jesus was a "Man of sorrows, and acquainted with grief" (Isaiah 53:3). Suffering disciples have the opportunity to learn the mind of the suffering Saviour.

4. Finally, I exhort all believers to keep up the habit of close communion with Christ, and never be afraid of "going too far" in your Christianity. Remember this, if you wish to have real peace in your times of illness. I believe that one reason why many have so little comfort either in health or in sickness is a lack of wholeheartedness in their faith. I believe that a half-hearted "keep-in-with-everybody" Christianity is offensive to God, and destroys true comfort in dying. The weakness and feebleness of such Christianity is most clearly seen during a period of illness.

If we want to have "strong consolation" in our time of need, we must not be content simply to be Christians. We must cultivate a heart-felt, experiential relationship with him. When medicine can do no more and nothing remains for us but to die, what will support us then? What will enable us then to feel, "I fear no evil"? (Psalm 23:4) Nothing - nothing at all - can do it, except close communion with Christ. Christ living in our hearts by faith, Christ putting his right arm under our heads, Christ felt to be sitting by our side - Christ alone can give us complete victory in our last struggle.

Let us hold more closely to Christ, love him more, live for him more thoroughly, confess him more boldly, follow him more fully. This kind of Christianity will bring its own reward. Worldly people may laugh at it. Weak Christians may think it extreme. Don't worry! In illness it will bring peace. In the world to come it will bring a crown of glory that does not fade away.

The time is short. The world is passing. A few more illnesses, and all will be over. A few more funerals and it will be *our* funeral. A few more storms and we shall be safe in the harbour. In the presence of Christ will be fullness of joy. God will wipe away all tears from his people's eyes.

Meanwhile, let us live the life of faith in the Son of God. He lives, though we may die. He lives, the One who abolished death and brought life and immortality to light by the gospel. One day he will change our lowly body and make it like his glorious body. In illness and in health, in life and in death, let us lean confidently on the Lord Jesus Christ.

14.
THE FAMILY OF GOD

"The whole family in heaven and earth." - Ephesians 3:15

Family gatherings are good. Nothing unites people like belonging to the same family, and anything which keeps up this family feeling is good. It is certainly natural and right to have family gatherings whenever possible. But a family gathering can be a sad time. As the years go by, "the whole family" is not often able to gather together. Younger members may be far away from home, and older members may have died. There are gaps in the family circle.

There is a family to which I want all who read this book to belong. It is far more important than any family on earth. It is the family of God. Let me tell you about it.

1. What this family is

What is this family? It is made up of all real Christians throughout the world. Belonging to this family does not depend upon earthly parents: you can only belong to this family by being born again of the Holy Spirit.

Why is this world-wide company of Christians called a family? First, because they all have *one Father*. They are all children of God. They all have the Spirit of adoption (Romans 8:15). They really mean it when they pray, "Our Father in heaven". Secondly, they are called a family because they all rejoice in *one name* - the name of their Elder Brother, the Lord

Jesus Christ. Thirdly, they are called a family because there is a strong *family likeness* between them. They resemble one another spiritually, as the sons and daughters of the Lord Almighty. They are all led by one Spirit. They all hate sin, and love God. They all trust in Christ and have no confidence in themselves. They love the same Bible and the same Throne of Grace. They all separate themselves from the world. They have the same inward experience of repentance, faith, hope, love, and humility. They experience the same kind of inward conflicts.

I want to emphasise the significance of this family likeness. It is very remarkable. People come from different nationalities and widely different educational and cultural backgrounds. Yet they can feel at home with one another in the space of a few minutes. Often they feel more at home with a Christian from a completely different culture, whom they have only just met, than with someone they have known for years who is not a Christian! God's people truly are a family! It is this family that we are considering now, and I want you to belong to it, because outside it there is no salvation.

2. The present position of this family

What is the present position of this family? It is divided into two parts: some are in heaven, and some are on earth. Although they belong to each other, at present they are completely separated. Those in heaven are at rest. They have finished their course; they have fought their battle; they have done their work. They are no longer troubled by sin and temptation, and are perfectly happy in the presence of Christ himself. Those on earth are still running their race, fighting their warfare, doing their work. They still have to strive against sin, resist the devil, and put to death their sinful desires. Yet these two parts still belong together, and the difference between them is only one of degree.

Both parts of the family love the same Saviour, and delight in the same perfect will of God, even though the part on earth does not do these things perfectly. Both parts are holy, though not in the same degree. Both parts are alike God's children, though one part is still learning, and sometimes needs to be taught with the rod and discipline. Both parts of the family are alike God's soldiers. Those on earth are still in the battle, and need the whole armour of God, whereas those in heaven are triumphant and beyond the reach of the enemy. Finally, both parts of this family are perfectly safe and secure. Christ cares as much for those on earth as for those in heaven, and has said plainly that "they shall never perish, neither shall anyone snatch them out of my hand" (John 10:28).

You see then that it would be a great mistake to judge God's family only by what you can see at present. You see only a small part of it. You cannot see the huge number of those who arc already in heaven. When the whole family is assembled at the last day, it will be "a multitude which no one could number" (Revelation 7:9). God's family is far richer and more glorious than you suppose, and I want you to belong to it.

3. What the future holds for this family

No one can ever predict the future of our earthly families. We "do not know what a day may bring forth" (Proverbs 27:1). But this family is different, for its future is certain, and not only certain, but good and happy.

One day, all the members of God's family will be brought safely home. On earth they are scattered, and tried and tested with afflictions. But none of them will perish (John 10:28). Every one of them will arrive home safely.

One day, all the members of God's family will have glorious bodies. When Christ comes the second time, the dead will be raised and the living will be changed. Every member will have a glorious body like that of the Lord.

One day, all the members of God's family will be gathered together in one company. It will make no difference where they have lived and died on earth. They will all meet together, to part no more.

One day, all the members of God's family will be united in mind and judgment. At present they are not agreed about everything. They all agree about the great central matters of salvation, but on many other matters they sadly disagree. But then, all disagreements will be swallowed up in perfect harmony.

One day, all the members of God's family will be perfected in holiness. Now, they all fall short in so many things. Then, they will all be "without spot, or wrinkle, or any such thing".

One day, all the members of God's family will be eternally provided for. They will all enter into the inheritance reserved for them. None will be passed over or forgotten.

These prospects for God's family are great realities. Think about them well. There is no earthly family with such a future!

Conclusion

Let me close with some words of application. May God bless them to the good of your soul!

1. I ask you this question: *Do you belong to the family of God?* I am not asking if you are a Baptist, or an Anglican, or belong to some other church. I am asking if you belong to *God's* family. If not, I invite you today to join it at once. Repent today. Seek Christ at once. Come and believe on him, and commit your soul to him today.

2. If you already belong to God's family, I want to encourage you to *think about your great privileges and learn to be more thankful.* What a privilege it is to have something which the world can neither give nor take away. Soon, our human family gatherings will be a thing of the past. But the gathering of God's family will be for ever. We should think much about it, and be thankful. The joy of that gathering will make up for

all that we may have suffered as Christians on earth.

Meanwhile, let us all strive to live in a way worthy of the family to which we belong. Let us do nothing to bring the family name into dishonour. Rather, let us commend it by our lives, and perhaps God will use our witness to cause others to say, "We will go with you."

15.
HEIRS OF GOD

"For as many as are led by the Spirit of God, these are sons of God. For you did not receive the spirit of bondage again to fear, but you received the Spirit of adoption by whom we cry out, 'Abba, Father.' The Spirit himself bears witness with our spirit that we are children of God, and if children, then heirs - heirs of God and joint heirs with Christ, if indeed we suffer with him, that we may also be glorified together." - *Romans 8:14-17*

The people Paul is writing about in these verses are the richest people on earth. They have the only inheritance really worth having - an inheritance with which no one is ever dissatisfied or disappointed. And unlike earthly inheritances which must be left behind at death, this inheritance can be kept for ever. Yet it is within the reach of everyone! It is available to everyone without exception who is prepared to receive it on God's terms.

Do you desire to share in this inheritance? The way to have it is to belong to the family of true Christians, for this is the family to which the inheritance belongs. If you are not a child of God already, I want to persuade you to become one today. If at present you have only a vague hope that you are a Christian, I want to persuade you to make absolutely sure of your relationship to God. Remember that only God's true children will share the inheritance!

1. The relationship which all true Christians have to God

True Christians are "sons of God". To be called a servant or a friend of God would be a great privilege, but there is nothing higher than to be called a son. It is commonly thought a great advantage and privilege to be a son of somebody great, but how much better it is to be a son of the King of kings and Lord of lords!

How can sinful men like us ever become sons of God? We are certainly not sons of God by nature. Men only become sons of God when his Spirit leads them to believe on Jesus Christ for salvation. The Bible says, "You are all children of God *by faith in Christ Jesus*" (Galatians 3:26). It is faith alone which unites us to Christ, and entitles us to be called "sons of God".

I want to emphasise this point. Even though the sons of God are chosen from all eternity and predestined for adoption as sons, it is not until they are called by God at a point in time, and exercise faith in Christ, that they actually become God's sons. The angels of God rejoice over the sinner who repents and believes. But they do not rejoice *until* he repents and believes, for only then does he become part of God's family.

We must not be deceived about this. I know that there is a sense in which God is the Father of all mankind. He created us all, and *in that sense* he is our Father, whether we are Christians or pagans. "In him we live and move and have our being" and "we are his offspring" (Acts 17:28). I know too that God loves all mankind with a love of pity and compassion. "His mercy is over all his works" (Psalm 145:9). But I utterly deny that God is *a reconciled and forgiving Father* to any except those who believe in the Lord Jesus Christ. God's holiness and justice are against such an idea, for they make it impossible for sinful people to approach God except through the Mediator. No one should comfort himself that God is his Father unless he has faith in the Lord Jesus Christ.

No one ought to think that such teaching is narrow-minded or harsh. The Gospel sets an open door before everyone. Its requirements are clear and simple. It says to *everyone*, "Believe on the Lord Jesus Christ and you will be saved." No one is excluded. But what about proud people who will not submit to Christ, and worldly people who are determined to go their own way and keep their sins? These are certainly not sons of God. God is *willing* to be their Father - but on certain distinct terms. They must come to him through Christ. They must commit their souls to him and give him their hearts. If men will not comply with those terms, how can they call God their Father? Such people are demanding that God should be their Father on *their* terms! They want Christ as their Saviour on *their* conditions! What could be more proud or unreasonable? We must reject such ideas, and hold fast to the teaching of the Bible. No one is a son of God except through Christ. And no one has a share in Christ except through faith.

I earnestly wish I did not have to emphasise this point so much. But I must, because of false teaching which is very popular. This false teaching speaks only about God's mercy and love. It ignores his holiness and justice. It never speaks about hell. It regards everyone as being saved. It talks about faith, but empties the word of all its biblical meaning. Everybody who believes anything is regarded as having faith. It talks about the Holy Spirit, but regards everybody as having the Spirit. Everybody is right, and nobody is wrong! It tells us that the Bible is an old-fashioned and very imperfect book, and you can believe as much of it as you want, and no more!

I most solemnly warn you to beware of such teaching. *Facts* are against it. Sodom and Gomorrah lie submerged under the waters of the Dead Sea, because of the judgment of God. The place where Babylon once stood is now utter desolation, because of the judgment of God. *Man's conscience* is against such teaching. It does not bring peace to a guilty conscience. *The biblical teaching about heaven* is against such teaching. Imagine a heaven in which the holy and the unholy, the pure and the impure, the good and the bad were all gathered together in one place. Imagine a heaven where Abraham and the

Sodomites, Peter and Judas Iscariot must live together for ever! Such a heaven would be no better than hell! *Concern for holiness and morality* testifies against such teaching. If everyone is a child of God, regardless of how he lives, and everyone is on his way to heaven, then what is the point of striving after holiness at all? *The Bible* is against such teaching from beginning to end. But this false teaching completely rejects the authority of the Bible, though it has nothing to offer in its place. Dear reader, I appeal to you: Beware of this false teaching. Hold fast to the truth plainly taught in God's word. There is no glorious inheritance for anyone who is not a son of God. And no one is a son of God without personal faith in the Lord Jesus Christ.

Do you *want to know whether you are a son of God*? Then ask yourself whether you have repented and believed in Jesus. Are you united in heart to Christ? If not, you are not a son of God. You are not born again. You are still in your sins. God is indeed your Creator, and in that sense your Father, but he is not your reconciled and forgiving Father in heaven.

Do you *desire to become a son of God*? If you see and feel your sins, and flee to Christ for salvation, then today you will be placed among God's children. Take hold of the hand which Christ holds out to you today, and you will become a son with all the privileges that involves. When you picked up this book you were a child of wrath. But tonight you will lie down a child of God. Old things will pass away and all things become new. Do you *truly* desire to be a son of God? Are you truly weary of your sins? Do you have something more than a lazy wish to be free? Then there is real comfort for you. Believe in the Lord Jesus Christ, and you will be saved and be a son of God.

Are you a true son of God already? Then rejoice, and be glad of your privileges. You have every reason to be thankful. "Behold what manner of love the Father has bestowed on us, that we should be called children of God!" (1 John 3:1) What if the world does not understand you? What if the world laughs at you? Let them laugh. God is your Father, and you have no need to be ashamed. There is no greater dignity than to be a son of God.

2. The evidences of this relationship with God.

How can someone be sure that he is a son of God? The verses of Scripture (Romans 8:14-17) which I am asking you to consider give us an answer to that question.

The sons of God are all *led by his Spirit* - "As many as are led by the Spirit of God, these are sons of God" (verse 14). The Holy Spirit is leading and teaching them all. He leads them away from sin, from self-righteousness and from the world. He leads them to Christ, to the Bible, to prayer and to holiness. From beginning to end, he is leading them. It is the Holy Spirit who leads them to Sinai, and convicts them of breaking God's law. It is the same Spirit who then leads them to Calvary, and shows them Christ dying for their sins. It is the Holy Spirit who shows them their own emptiness and also shows them something of the glory that is to come.

The sons of God all *have the feelings of adopted children towards their Father in heaven* - "You did not receive the spirit of bondage again to fear, but you received the Spirit of adoption by whom we cry out, 'Abba, Father'" (verse 15). By nature all are guilty and condemned, and have a slavish fear of God. But when they become sons of God, this changes. Instead of slavish fear, they have peace with God and confidence towards him as their heavenly Father. They know that the Lord Jesus Christ is their Peacemaker with God. They know that they can draw near to God with boldness and speak to him as their Father. The spirit of bondage and fear is exchanged for the Spirit of liberty and love. They are still conscious of being sinners, but they know they need not be afraid because they are clothed in the righteousness of the Lord Jesus Christ.

I admit that some Christians experience these feelings more than others. Some still experience the return of the old fears to trouble them. But few of God's children could not tell you that

112

since they have come to know Christ their feelings towards God have been very different from before.

The sons of God *have the witness of the Spirit in their consciences* - "The Spirit himself bears witness with our spirit that we are children of God" (verse 16). The sons of God have something in their hearts which tells them there is a relationship between them and God. The extent to which they possess this varies greatly. With some, it is a loud and clear testimony that they belong to Christ, and Christ to them. With others it is a feeble, stammering whisper, which the devil and the flesh often prevent them from hearing. Some of God's children enjoy great assurance, while others find it hard to believe that they have real faith. But in every real Christian there is something which he would never agree to give up. Even those who are tossed about with doubts and fears would never agree to give up that measure of hope which they do have in exchange for the easy life of a careless and worldly man.

The sons of God all *share in suffering with Christ* - "If children, then heirs — heirs of God and joint heirs with Christ, if indeed we suffer with him" (verse 17). All God's children experience trials and troubles for Christ. They experience trials from the world, from the flesh and from the devil. Often they are misunderstood or badly treated by friends and relatives. They may have to suffer slander or mockery. They may suffer for putting Christ before their earthly concerns. They also know the trials which arise from within their own sinful hearts. There are varying degrees of suffering. Some suffer more, and some less. Some suffer one way, and some another. But I do not believe that one child of God ever reached heaven without any suffering at all.

Suffering is part of the experience of all God's family. "Whom the Lord loves, he chastens" (Hebrews 12:6). "If you are without chastening ... then you are illegitimate and not sons" (Hebrews 12:8). Suffering is part of God's process of making us holy. His children are chastened to wean them away from the world and make them partakers of God's holiness. It is one of the badges of Christian discipleship. Christ himself was crucified and his disciples must also take up their cross.

Let me warn you, then, against believing that you are a son of God unless you have the scriptural marks of sonship. It is not enough that you have been baptised and are a member of a Christian church. The marks of sonship are given in the eighth chapter of Romans, and you have no reason to suppose that you are a son of God unless you have these marks.

3. **The privileges of this relationship**

True Christians are "heirs of God, and joint heirs with Christ". These words speak of a glorious prospect for all God's children. If it means much to be an heir of a rich person on earth, how much more does it mean to be a son and heir of the King of kings! But Christians are "joint heirs with Christ". They will share in his majesty and glory, when they are glorified together with him. And this is not for only a few Christians - it is for *all* the sons of God!

We know only a little of the inheritance which awaits God's people. The Bible does not tell us a great deal, for our minds could not take it in. But it tells us enough to bring us great comfort, and we do well to think about these things.

Do we find *knowledge* desirable? Is the little that we know about God and Christ precious to us? Do we long to know more? In glory, we will have that knowledge. "Then I shall know, just as I also am known" (1 Corinthians 13:12).

Do we find *holiness* desirable? Do we long for complete conformity to the image of God? In glory, we shall have it. Christ gave himself for the church, not only to sanctify it on earth, but also "that he might present it to himself a glorious church, not having spot or wrinkle or any such thing" (Ephesians 5:27).

Do we find *rest* desirable? Do we long for a world in which we need not be always watching and wrestling? In glory we shall have it. "There remains a rest for the people of God"

(Hebrews 4:9). Our daily, hourly conflict with the world, the flesh, and the devil will be ended for ever.

Do we find *service* desirable? Do we delight to work for Christ, though we are burdened by a feeble body? Do we often find our spirit willing, but our flesh weak? In glory we shall be able to serve perfectly, without any weariness. "They serve him day and night in his temple" (Revelation 7:15).

Do we find *satisfaction* desirable? Do we find the world empty? Do we long for the filling of every void in our hearts? In glory we shall have it perfectly. "I shall be satisfied when I awake in your likeness" (Psalm 17:15).

Do we find *fellowship with God's people* desirable? Do we feel that we are never as happy as when we are with God's people? In glory we shall be with them for ever. "The Son of Man will send out his angels, and they will gather out of his kingdom all things that offend, and those who practise lawlessness" (Matthew 13:41). "He will send his angels with a great sound of a trumpet, and they will gather together his elect from the four winds" (Matthew 24:31). Praise God! We shall be with the saints of God we read about in the Bible, whose example we have tried to follow. We shall be with men and women of whom the world was not worthy. We shall be with those we have known and loved in Christ on earth. We shall be with them for ever, never to part again.

Do we find *communion with Christ* desirable? Is his Name precious to us? Do our hearts warm within us at the thought of his dying love? In glory, we shall have perfect communion with Christ. "We shall always be with the Lord" (1 Thessalonians 4:17). We shall see him in his kingdom. Where he is, there the sons of God will be. When he sits down in his glory, they will sit by his side. What a blessed prospect is this! I am a dying man in a dying world. The world to come is largely unknown. But Christ is there! That is enough. If there is rest and peace in following Christ by faith on earth, how much more will there be when we see him face to face.

Are you not yet among the sons and heirs of God? Then I pity you with all my heart! You are missing so much, and your life is ultimately without purpose. Will you not hear the voice of Jesus and learn of him now?

If you *are* among God's sons and heirs, what cause you have to rejoice and be happy! Do not be over-concerned about your circumstances in this life. Your treasure is in heaven. Glory in your inheritance!

Conclusion

1. In conclusion, let me ask every reader, *Whose child are you?* Are you a child of nature, or a child of grace? Are you a child of the devil or a child of God? I appeal to you to settle the question without delay. How foolish to remain uncertain about such an important issue! The time is short. You are fast heading towards death and judgment. Do not give yourself any rest until you can say with assurance, "I know that I am a son of God!"

2. If you are a son of God, *I appeal to you to live in a way that is worthy of your Father's family.* Honour him in your life, by obeying his commandments and loving all his children. Live in this world as one who does not belong here, but is travelling to a home in glory. Let others see what a good and happy thing it is to be a son of God. Keep your eyes fixed on the Lord Jesus, remembering that apart from him you can do nothing, but with him you can do all things. (See John 15:5 and Philippians 4:13.) Watch and pray. The time will very soon come when you will hear the words: "Come, you blessed of my Father, inherit the kingdom prepared for you from the foundation of the world" (Matthew 25:34).

16.
THE GREAT GATHERING

"Concerning the coming of our Lord Jesus Christ and our gathering together to him." - 2 Thessalonians 2:1

Throughout the world, people love to gather together. Few people like to be alone, and most of us love those times when we can gather together with our families. But often there is something sad about earthly gatherings. They are over so quickly. Often there are memories of people who have died and can no longer gather with us. No earthly gathering brings us perfect and unmixed happiness. But, thank God, there is a better gathering still to come - a gathering where there will be joy without any sorrow, happiness without any tears. Let me tell you what I mean.

1. One day there will be a "gathering together" of true Christians

There will be a "gathering together" of true Christians on the day when the Lord Jesus Christ comes back to this world. "He will send his angels with a great sound of a trumpet, and they will gather together his elect from the four winds, from one end of heaven to the other" (Matthew 24:31). Christians who have died will be raised up, and those who are still alive will be changed. (See Revelation 20:13; 1 Thessalonians 4:16,17; 1 Corinthians 15:51,52.) It is then that all Christians who ever lived will be gathered together with the Lord Jesus.

The purpose of this gathering is partly for the final reward of Christ's people. Their complete justification from all guilt will be declared to the whole world; they will receive the "crown of glory that does not fade away" and be admitted publicly into the joy of their Lord. It is also partly for their safety, that they may be safely hidden in the day of God's righteous anger.

This will be a great gathering. Every believer will be there, from every age and every country. The weakest and feeblest will be there; none will be missing. Together they will make a multitude which no one could number.

This will be a wonderful gathering. People who never met in this world, who spoke different languages and came from completely different cultures, will all be together in perfect unity. We shall see some in heaven whom we would never have expected to be saved at all. And all will be praising the marvels of God's grace.

This will be a humbling gathering. It will put an end to all bigotry and intolerance for ever. All party spirit, lack of brotherly love, religious jealousy and pride will be overthrown for ever. There, at last, we shall all be "clothed with humility" (1 Peter 5:5).

This gathering ought to be frequently in our thoughts. When every other gathering is forgotten, only one question is really important: "Shall I be gathered with Christ's people, or be left behind to everlasting sorrow?" LET US TAKE CARE THAT WE ARE NOT LEFT BEHIND.

2. We should look forward to this "gathering together" with great pleasure

Why is this "gathering together" so desirable? Paul obviously thought it was something to which we should look forward with pleasure. Let me show you why.

This gathering will be in a state quite different from our present condition. In this world, God's children are scattered everywhere. Often they are isolated and lonely, and longing for more fellowship with those who love the Lord. There, they will all be together for ever!

This gathering will be an assembly entirely of one mind. There will be no hypocrites, such as mar the gatherings of believers on earth. There will be no controversies between believers. The graces of believers will be fully developed, and their besetting sins left behind. No wonder Paul tells us to look forward to this gathering!

This gathering will be a meeting from which no believer will be absent. The weakest lamb will not be left behind in the wilderness. The youngest will not be forgotten. We shall meet with Old Testament believers who believed in Christ before he came. We shall meet with those who knew Christ in his earthly life, and with all who have believed in him ever since, hearing from them about all that the Lord did for each of them. Will that not be sweet indeed?

This gathering will be a meeting without a parting. Here, there are no such meetings. The time always comes to say "Good-bye". But there, there will be no more old age, death or change. No wonder that Paul tells us to look forward to it!

Conclusion

I ask you now to give serious attention to this important subject. If you see nothing desirable in the gathering together I have been describing, you should certainly question whether you are a Christian at all.

1. I ask you a plain question: Will you be a part of this gathering, or will you be left behind? On that day mankind will be divided into two portions - those who are gathered together like wheat into Christ's barn, and those who are left like the weeds to be burned. In which portion will *you* be? It is not enough to say you are not sure, but you hope for the best. The Bible tells you plainly enough who will and who will not be gathered. Do not rest until you are sure!

2. I tell you a plain way of answering that question. Ask yourself this: What kind of gatherings do you like best on the earth? Do you love to gather together with God's people? If you take no delight in meeting true Christians on earth, how could you possibly delight in their company in heaven? Our tastes on earth are a sure evidence of the state of our hearts. The man who hopes to be gathered with God's saints in heaven when he loves only gatherings of sinners on the earth is deceiving himself completely. If he lives and dies like that, he will find at last that it would have been better never to have been born.

3. If you are a true Christian, I exhort you to be often looking forward to this gathering. The day after a great victory in battle is often a sorrowful time, for the joy of victory is marred by the loss of those who have died. But on that great day, the soldiers of Christ's army will all be present to answer the last roll call. Their number will be as complete as before the battle. Not one believer will be missing in this great "gathering together". In the present world you may often be sad and lonely, finding few to pray with, to open your heart to, and to exchange experiences with. Remember that this will soon be over, and look forward eagerly to the "coming of our Lord Jesus Christ and our gathering together to him".

17.
THE GREAT SEPARATION

"His winnowing fan is in his hand, and he will thoroughly purge his threshing-floor, and gather his wheat into the barn; but he will burn up the chaff with unquenchable fire." - Matthew 3:12

These words were spoken by John the Baptist about the Lord Jesus Christ. They have not yet been fulfilled, but one day they will be. Let us consider their significance under four headings.

1. Mankind is divided into two great classes

These words remind us that although men divide society into many classes, God sees only two. Here they are called the wheat and the chaff. God, who sees the hearts of everyone, puts everyone into one of these categories.

Who are the wheat? The wheat means Christians - those who believe in the Lord Jesus, love him and live for him. Although they are sinful and unworthy in their own eyes, they are precious in God's eyes.

Who are the chaff? The chaff means all those, without exception, who do not have saving faith in Christ and are not sanctified by the Holy Spirit. It does not matter whether they are open unbelievers, or whether they call themselves Christians. If they have no living faith and are not holy, then they are chaff. They may have great natural gifts, and have great influence in the world. But because they neglect God's salvation, God takes no pleasure in them.

It is important to realise that there is no third class of men. In the days of the great Flood, there were only two classes of men - those in the ark and those outside. The Lord Jesus speaks of two ways - the broad way that leads to destruction and the narrow way that leads to life. There is no other way. So I have to ask you plainly: Are you wheat, or are you chaff? Are you a new creature? Have you repented? Are you trusting in Christ? Do you love and serve him? Do you love the Bible, and wrestle in prayer? Are you a Christian at work, and at home, on weekdays as well as Sundays? However unpleasant it may be, I ask you to face these questions now. If you are chaff, it will be better to discover it now, while you still have time to repent.

2. The two great classes of mankind will be separated

Our text also tells us that there is a time when the two great classes of mankind will be separated. One day Christ will do what the farmer does to his corn: he will separate the wheat from the chaff. This has not happened yet. At present, the wheat and the chaff mix together, even among those who call themselves Christians. Men cannot always distinguish between them, for we cannot read other people's hearts. Until Christ comes again, churches will always have chaff among the wheat. And until Christ comes, there will certainly be both wheat and chaff in the world. But when Christ comes, what a great separation there will be! The wheat will form one company - all of them godly. The chaff will form another - all of them ungodly. And between the two there will be a great gulf that no one can pass over. The one company will be completely blessed. The other will be completely miserable.

If you are a true Christian, you love the company of God's saints, and the company of worldly people is a great trial to you. You ought to long for the time when Christ will come again. Then, God's people will all be gathered together forever, never to be separated again.

Am I speaking to someone who knows that his heart is not

right in the sight of God? You should fear and tremble at the thought of Christ's coming. It will show you up as you really are. God will never be deceived. I urge you to tremble - and to repent!

3. What Christ's people will receive

Our text tells us that Christ "will gather his wheat into the barn". Let me show you what his people will receive when he comes to cleanse his floor. He will gather all his believing people into a place of safety. Not a single sinner who put his faith in Christ for salvation will be missing. Every grain of wheat will be there. We do not appreciate as we ought just how much the Lord cares for his people. Let me try to show you.

The Lord *takes pleasure* in his believing people. Their weaknesses and failures do not break the union between him and them. He knew all their weaknesses when he chose them. He will never break his covenant and cast them off. When they fall, he will raise them up again. When they stray, he will bring them back. Their prayers are pleasant to him, just as the stammering efforts of a child are pleasing to its father, and he is pleased by their efforts to serve him.

The Lord cares for his believing people in their *lives*. All the circumstances of their lives are under his control. Angels minister to them; the Father, Son and Holy Spirit are present with them; none can touch them without his permission; and all things work together for their good. He only afflicts them for their good, and he only prunes them to make them more fruitful.

The Lord cares for his believing people in their *deaths*. Their times are in his hand. They are kept till they are ripe for glory, and no longer. No disease can take them away, till the Lord gives his word, and when that word is given no doctor can keep them alive. When they are dying, the everlasting arms are around them, and when they depart it is to be with Christ. What a contrast with the unbeliever! For the unbeliever, death closes the door on his last opportunity, and shuts him out from hope for ever, but for the believer death opens the door of heaven that he may enter in.

The Lord *will care* for his believing people in the dreadful day of his appearing. The voice of the archangel and the trumpet of God will not terrify them. The fire will not touch them. They will be "caught up to meet the Lord in the air" (1 Thessalonians 4:17). It is a blessed thing to be Christ's wheat!

I am amazed, when I think about Christ's care for his people, that anyone can deny that Christ keeps each of his people safe to the end. How could he love them enough to die for them, yet subsequently let them be cast away? Suppose you had been present at a shipwreck and seen a helpless child about to drown, and had risked your own life by plunging in and bringing him to the shore. Would you simply lay him on the land, cold and unconscious, and do nothing more for him? No! You would take him in your arms to the nearest house. You would do everything you could to restore him to health. You would not think of leaving him till you were sure of his recovery. And can you think that the Lord Jesus is less compassionate? By no means! Those he loves, he loves to the end. He never leaves or forsakes them. He finishes the work he has begun.

A man who has truly experienced God's grace can never fall from it. If he commits sin, he will be brought to repentance as Peter was. If he turns aside from the path of righteousness, he will be brought back like David. It is not his own strength that keeps him. He has been chosen by God the Father. Christ intercedes for him. The love of the Holy Spirit holds him. The three Persons of the Holy Trinity are committed to his salvation.

If you are not a disciple of Christ, consider what privileges you are missing - peace with God now, and glory in the future! Will you not be wise and seek him now?

If you feel you are a weak disciple, do not suppose that your weakness will shut you out from any of these great privileges.

What is important is that your faith should be *true* faith, even if it is weak. Do not fear. Do not be discouraged. The babies in a family are as much loved as the older brothers and sisters. It is the same in Christ's family. All are loved and cared for. All will be gathered safely home at last.

4. What will happen to those who are not Christ's people

Our text tells us that Christ will "burn up the chaff with unquenchable fire". Let me show you what will happen to those who are not Christ's people. Christ will punish with fearful punishment all who are not his disciples - all who are found impenitent and unbelieving; all who have clung to sin and to the world, and set their affections on earthly things. Their punishment will be *severe*. Jesus speaks of burning. It will be *eternal*. He says the fire is unquenchable. These are not things I like to speak about. But God's Word speaks about them, and we must take heed.

I know that there are some who do not believe there is such a place as hell. Such people are telling men just what the devil first told Adam and Eve: "You will not die!" (Genesis 3:4) There are others who do not believe that hell is eternal. These also do the devil's work, for they are really saying to people, "Don't worry too much about it. It is not for ever!" There are others who believe there is a hell, but never seem to think that anybody is going there. Others believe there is a hell, and yet never like it to be spoken about. These also do the devil's work, for he rejoices when Christians are silent about hell.

But we are not concerned with what men think. We are concerned with what God has told us in his Word. Do you believe the Bible? If so, you can be sure of these facts:

First, hell is *real*. The Bible teaches this as clearly as it teaches that Christ died on the cross for sinners. If you reject its teaching on hell, there is no biblical teaching you can safely believe. You might as well throw your Bible away.

Secondly, hell will *not be empty*. The same Saviour who now sits on a throne of grace will one day sit on a throne of judgment. The same Lord who now says, "Come to me" will one day say, "Depart from me", and "these will go away into everlasting punishment" (Matthew 25:46).

Thirdly, hell will be *a place of intense sorrow and suffering*. Some say the pictures Jesus uses are figures of speech - the worm, the fire, the darkness, the gnashing of teeth. Perhaps they are. But they mean something. They speak of miseries of mind and conscience far worse than those of the body.

Fourthly, hell is *eternal*. If it is not, then words have no meaning, for the Bible uses expressions like "for ever and ever", "everlasting", "unquenchable", and "never-dying". If it were not eternal, the whole gospel would be undermined. If someone may eventually be released from hell without faith in Christ, or sanctification by the Spirit, then sin is no longer an infinite evil, and there was no need for Christ to atone for it. It must be eternal or it would cease to be hell, for one of the features of hell is that it is utterly without hope.

Fifthly, hell is *a subject which we must speak about*. The Bible speaks about it, and no one spoke about it more than the Lord Jesus Christ did. So we cannot keep silent about it. It is our duty to warn men of their danger. If a man's house were on fire, it would be our duty to shout, "Fire!" In the same way, we must warn people of the reality of hell.

I appeal to every reader, beware of false views on this subject. Beware of inventing your own god - a god who is all love without holiness, a god who will not separate the good from the bad in eternity. Such a god is an invention of your own. He does not exist. He is not the God of the Bible.

Beware of picking and choosing which parts of the Bible you will believe. You must take the Bible as it is. You must read it all, and believe it all. You must come to it like a little child, and say, "Speak, Lord, for your servant hears."

Conclusion

In conclusion, let me urge upon you four things.

1. Realise that these things are real and true. Try to realise the seriousness of them, and live as one who believes that they are true.

2. Realise that these things concern *you*. They are not only about other people. *You* are either among the wheat or the chaff. *You* will one day be either in heaven or in hell.

3. Realise that - if you desire to be found among the wheat - the Lord Jesus Christ is willing to receive you. Jesus wishes his barn to be filled with wheat! He is bringing many sons to glory! He wept over unbelieving Jerusalem. He invites *you* through my words right now. He says plainly, "I have no pleasure in the death of the wicked, but that the wicked turn from his way and live. Turn, turn from your evil ways! For why should you die?" (Ezekiel 33:1) Why should *you* not come to him *now* - right now? If you are determined to cling to your sins and to the world, I have fairly warned you. There is only one end for you, and that is in the unquenchable fire. But if you are willing to be saved, the Lord Jesus is ready to save you. "Come to me, weary soul," he says, "and I will give you rest. Come, guilty and sinful soul, and I will give you free pardon. Come, lost and ruined soul, and I will give you eternal life". (See Matthew 11:28.)

4. Realise that if you have committed your soul to Christ, he will never allow you to perish. The everlasting arms are around you. The hand that was nailed to the cross is holding you. The wisdom that designed the world is committed to keeping you safe. Your faith may be small, but all that matters is that it is real. Cast all your cares upon Jesus. He loves to be trusted. If you are among Christ's wheat now, you will certainly be gathered into his barn when he comes again.

18.
ETERNITY

"The things which are seen are temporary, but the things which are not seen are eternal." - 2 Corinthians 4:18

Eternity is one of the most solemn subjects in the Word of God. Our mortal minds can never wholly understand it, but God has spoken about it in his Word, and we must pay close attention to what God has said. I feel deeply my own inadequacy to handle this subject, but I pray that God himself will bless what I write, and plant the seeds of eternal life in the hearts of many readers. Let me speak to you under four headings.

1. Everything in this world is temporary

First, I want you to consider that we live in a world where everything is temporary. Everything around us is decaying, dying, coming to an end. Whatever our present condition in life, we too will soon be gone. *Beauty* is only temporary. Sarah was once a very beautiful woman, yet the day came when even Abraham her husband said, "Let me bury my dead out of my sight" (Genesis 23:4). *Strength of body* is only temporary. David was once a great warrior, yet the day came when even David had to be nursed and cared for in his old age like a child.

This is a humbling and painful truth, but we must pay attention to it. It is a truth to challenge you if you are living only for this world. Will you not wake up to the fact that the things for which you are living are all temporary? Your recreations and pleasures, your business and profits, will soon be over, along with everything else on which you have set your heart and mind. You cannot keep these things. You will not be able to take them with you. The world is passing away. Will you not listen to what God has said? "Set your mind on things above, not on things on the earth" (Colossians 3:2). "The world is passing away, and the lust of it; but he who does the will of God abides forever" (1 John 2:17).

If you are a true Christian, however, the same truth ought to cheer and comfort you. All your trials and conflicts are temporary. They will soon be at an end. Bear them patiently, and look beyond them. Your cross will soon be exchanged for a crown, and you will sit down with Abraham and Isaac and Jacob in the kingdom of God.

2. Everything in the world to come is eternal

Secondly, I want you to consider that we are all going towards a world where everything is eternal. In this respect the unseen world which lies beyond the grave is completely different from this world. Whether it is happy or miserable, a condition of joy or of sorrow, it is for ever. "The things which are not seen are eternal." It is almost impossible for our minds to grasp what this involves. But the Bible speaks about it, and we must listen.

Let us be quite clear in our minds that the *future happiness* of the saved is eternal. The inheritance of God's people is "incorruptible and undefiled and does not fade away" (1 Peter 1:4). They "receive the crown of glory that does not fade away" (1 Peter 5:4). At God's "right hand are pleasures for evermore" (Psalm 16:11). Their warfare is finished, their fight is over, and their work is done. They shall hunger no more, nor thirst any more. God's people are travelling towards a home which shall never be broken up, a family gathering without a separation, a day without a night. They shall be "always with the Lord" (1 Thessalonians 4:17).

Let us be equally clear that the *future misery* of those who are lost is also eternal. This is an awful truth, which we naturally shrink from thinking about. But it is plainly revealed in Scripture, and I dare not keep quiet about it. Eternal happiness and eternal misery stand side by side. The duration of the one is the same as the duration of the other. Heaven is eternal, and so is hell. The joy of the believer is eternal, and so is the misery of the lost.

Those who think that future punishment is not eternal like to talk about God's love, and to tell us that eternal punishment would contradict the mercy and compassion of God. But no one was ever so loving, merciful and compassionate as the Lord Jesus Christ. Yet he is the One who speaks about "the worm that never dies and the fire that is not quenched" (Mark 9:48). He is the One who speaks about the wicked going away into "everlasting punishment" and the righteous into "everlasting life" (Matthew 25:46[1]). Everyone knows the Apostle Paul's great passage about love in 1 Corinthians 13. Yet it is the same apostle who says that the wicked "shall be punished with everlasting destruction" (2 Thessalonians 1:9). The Apostle John writes much about Christian love in his Gospel and Letters. Yet it is the same apostle who wrote the book of Revelation, which emphasises so strongly the reality and eternity of future punishment.

We dare not think we know better than the Bible about this matter. Mankind fell into sin when they believed Satan's lie, "You will not surely die" (Genesis 3:4). Satan still deceives men with the same lie today. He persuades men that they may live and die in sin, and yet at some future period they may be saved. Let us not be ignorant of his devices. Let us hold fast to the truth of God's Word. God has revealed that the happiness of the saved is eternal, and that the misery of the lost is eternal also.

If we do not hold this awful truth, we *strike at the heart of biblical Christianity*. What was the point of God's Son becoming man, agonising in Gethsemane, and dying on the cross for

[1]The same Greek word is used to describe the duration of the punishment and the life.

130

our sins, if men could finally be saved without believing on him? But there is not the slightest suggestion in the Bible that saving faith in Christ can begin after death. And what need is there for the work of the Holy Spirit if sinners could enter heaven at last without conversion and a new heart? But there is not the smallest amount of evidence that anyone can be born again and have a new heart after he has died without Christ. If a man could escape eternal punishment without faith in Christ or sanctification by the Holy Spirit, then sin would no longer be an infinite evil, and there would have been no need for Christ to make atonement for it.

If we do not hold this truth, we *encourage people to continue in sin*. Why should men repent and take up the cross if they can live and die in sin but still get into heaven at last?

If we do not believe in the eternity of punishment, we *cannot consistently believe in the eternity of heaven*. They stand or fall together. The same language is used in the Bible about both.

I leave this part of my subject with a deep sense of its painfulness. It is a hard subject to handle lovingly, yet if we believe the Bible we must never give up any of its teaching. Men may talk about God's mercy, love and compassion, and ignore his holiness and purity, his justice, his unchangeableness and hatred of sin. We must be careful not to fall into this error. We must believe in God as he is. We must believe in what he has revealed about himself.

In Psalm 145:8-20 we have the most beautiful description of God's mercy. "The LORD is gracious and full of compassion, slow to anger and great in mercy. The LORD is good to all, and his tender mercies are over all his works." "The LORD upholds all who fall, and raises up all who are bowed down." "The LORD is righteous in all his ways, gracious in all his works. The LORD is near to all who call upon him, to all who call upon him in truth. The LORD preserves all who love him." How striking it is, then, to read what follows: "But all the wicked he will destroy."

3. Our state in eternity will depend upon what we are now

Thirdly, I want you to consider that our state in eternity depends entirely upon what we are in time. Our lives in this world are very short. "What is your life? It is even a vapour that appears for a little time and then vanishes away" (James 4:14). Yet although our earthly life is so short, our condition in the endless eternity to come depends upon it. The Bible says that God "will render to each one according to his deeds: eternal life to those who by patient continuance in doing good seek for glory, honour, and immortality; but to those who are self-seeking and do not obey the truth, but obey unrighteousness - indignation and wrath" (Romans 2:6-8).

We ought never to forget that this life is a state of probation for us all. Each day we are sowing seeds which will grow and bear fruit. There are eternal consequences resulting from all our thoughts, words and actions. "For every idle word men may speak, they will give account of it in the day of judgment" (Matthew 12:36). Paul says, "He who sows to his flesh will of the flesh reap corruption, but he who sows to the Spirit will of the Spirit reap everlasting life" (Galatians 6:8). What we sow in this life we shall reap after death, and that to all eternity.

The Bible plainly teaches that the condition in which we die is the condition in which we shall rise when the last trumpet sounds. There is no repentance in the grave. There is no conversion after death. Now is the time to believe in Christ, and lay hold on eternal life. Now is the time to turn from darkness to light, and to make our calling and election sure. If we leave this world without having repented and believed in Christ, we shall find that it would have been better for us if we had never been born.

In the light of this, how carefully we ought to use our time! Remember that your hours and days, weeks and years, are all adding up to an eternal condition beyond the grave. Remember this especially in using the means of grace. Never be careless about your daily prayers and Bible reading, your use of the

Lord's Day, your attitude when worshipping in church. Remember this also when you are tempted to do evil. Satan will whisper, "This is only a little sin. There will be no harm in it. Everyone else does it." But you must look beyond time, to the unseen world of eternity, and view temptation in the light of its eternal consequences.

4. We must look to Christ alone both for time and eternity

Fourthly, I want you to consider that the Lord Jesus Christ is the great Friend to whom we must all look for help, both for time and for eternity. We can never proclaim too fully or too loudly the purpose for which Christ came into the world. He came to give us hope and peace while we live among "the things which are temporary", and to give us glory and blessedness when we go to live among "the things which are eternal". Through him a mortal man may pass through the "things which are temporary" with comfort, and look forward to the "things which are eternal" without fear.

These privileges were purchased for us at the cost of Christ's own blood. He became our substitute and bore our sins in his own body on the cross, and rose again for our justification. He "suffered once for sins, the just for the unjust, that he might bring us to God" (1 Peter 3:18). The One who was sinless was punished for our sins, that we poor sinful creatures might have pardon and justification while we live, and glory and blessedness when we die.

All these things which Christ has purchased are freely available to everyone who will turn from his sins, come to him and believe. "If anyone thirsts, let him come to me and drink" (John 7:37). "The one who comes to me I will by no means cast out" (John 6:37). "Believe on the Lord Jesus Christ, and you will be saved" (Acts 16:31). "Whoever believes in him shall not perish but have everlasting life" (John 3:16).

The person who has Christ can look around him at the "things which are temporary" without being dismayed. He has treasure in heaven, where neither moth nor rust can destroy, nor thieves break in and steal (Matthew 6:20). He can look forward to the "things which are eternal" without being alarmed. His Saviour has risen and gone to prepare a place for him. When he leaves this world he will have a crown of glory and be for ever with the Lord. But let us all be perfectly clear in our minds that there is only one way to experience this. We must have Christ as our Saviour and Friend. We must lay hold of Christ by faith, and as long as we live in this body we must live a life of faith in the Son of God (Galatians 2:20). How happy is the man or woman who truly believes in Christ! When John Knox, the Scottish Reformer, was dying and could no longer speak, a servant asked him to raise his hand as a sign that the gospel he had preached in life was now giving him comfort in death. The dying man heard, and raised his hand three times. Then he was gone. I say again, happy is the man or woman who believes in the Lord Jesus! If you and I are without comfort now and have no hope for the future, the fault is entirely our own. It is because we "are not willing to come to Christ that we may have life" (John 5:40).

Conclusion

I finish with four questions, to help you examine yourself.

1. First, *how are you using your time?* Life is very short and uncertain. It will soon be over, and that forever. What are you doing about your immortal soul? Are you wasting your time, or using it wisely? Are you preparing to meet God?

2. Secondly, *where will you be in eternity?* Eternity will soon - very soon - be upon you. Where will you be then? Will you be among the lost or among the saved? Oh, give yourself no rest until your soul is safe! It is a fearful thing to die unprepared, and fall into the hands of the living God.

3. Thirdly, *do you desire to be safe both in time and eternity?* Then seek Christ, and believe in him. Come to him just as you are. Seek him while he may be found. Call upon him

134

while he is near. It is not too late. He waits to have mercy on you. Before the door is shut and the judgment begins, repent, believe and be saved.

4. Fourthly, *Do you desire to be happy?* Then cling to Christ, and live the life of faith in him. Follow him with all your heart and soul and mind and strength. Seek to know him better every day. If you do this, you will have great peace while you pass through the present world, and will be able to look forward to the unseen world to come with unfailing confidence. You will be able to feel and know that "if our earthly house, this tent, is destroyed, we have a building from God, a house not made with hands, eternal in the heavens" (2 Corinthians 5:1).

APPENDIX

THE LORD'S DAY

"Remember the Sabbath Day, to keep it holy." - Exodus 20:8
"I was in the Spirit on the Lord's Day." - Revelation 1:10

The subject of the Lord's Day is one about which there is much confusion among Christians. Many are not clear whether God has appointed a special day of rest and worship for Christians or not. They are not sure whether it is right or wrong to work or to engage in sports on Sunday. Yet the subject is one of immense importance. The well-being of the church is intimately connected with the Lord's Day, and I want to examine three points in connection with it.

1. The authority of the Lord's Day

Let us first consider the question, What is our authority for observing the Lord's Day? Many Christians think that the Lord's Day is simply a day which the church itself has chosen for worship, and that it has no authority in the Word of God. They see it as having no connection with the Old Testament sabbath. They think that the principle that one day in every seven should be completely set apart for God was a purely Jewish ordinance which has no place in the Christian life.

I believe that such Christians are quite wrong. I firmly believe that the setting apart of one day in seven is *part of the eternal law of God*. It is one of the everlasting rules which God has revealed for the guidance of all mankind. It is quite true that since the resurrection of Christ Christians have observed the first day of the week and not the seventh, but that has not changed in the least degree the great principle that *one day in seven belongs to God*. Let me try to show you the importance of this principle from God's Word.

a. Turn first to *the history of creation*. There we read that "God blessed the seventh day and sanctified it" (Genesis 2:3). Right at the beginning of history we have the principle that one day in seven is set apart for God. This was before man fell into sin, and before there ever was a Jewish nation. Surely this reveals God's will that this principle is for all mankind in every generation.

b. Turn now to *the giving of the Law on Mount Sinai*. It is extremely important to realise that there is a clear distinction between the Ten Commandments and the rest of Moses' law. Only the Ten Commandments were spoken in the hearing of all the people. Then, after God had spoken them, the Bible expressly says, "And he added no more" (Deuteronomy 5:22). Of course, God added many more commandments for the people of Israel, but he added no more *of the same kind as the Ten Commandments*. The giving of the Ten Commandments was accompanied by thunder, lightning and an earthquake, to emphasise their uniqueness and importance. Only the Ten Commandments were written on tablets of stone by God himself. Only the Ten Commandments were put inside the Ark of the Covenant. In all these ways God made it clear that the Ten Commandments were different from all the other laws given through Moses.

Now it cannot be denied that nine of these Commandments deal with *moral* matters. They deal with principles which are valid for all mankind in every generation. And it is among these commandments that we find the law of the sabbath. By placing his sabbath law among such commandments, God was surely declaring that it is the same *kind* of commandment as these others. Moreover, we find that of all the Ten Commandments, the law of the sabbath is the longest, fullest and most detailed. In the light of these facts, I cannot believe that God intended the sabbath principle to be only temporary.

c. Turn now to *the writings of the Old Testament Prophets*. We find the prophets speaking repeatedly about the breaking of the sabbath commandment side by side with terrible transgressions of the moral law (See, for example, Ezekiel 20:13,16,24 and 22:8,26.) We find them speaking of it as one of the great sins which brought judgment on Israel and carried the Jews into captivity (See Nehemiah 13:18 and Jeremiah 17:19-27.) It seems clear, therefore, that they regarded the observance of the sabbath as being in a quite different category from the observance of the ceremonial law. This strongly suggests that the sabbath principle was not to be abolished along with the ceremonial law.

d. Turn now to *the teaching of our Lord Jesus Christ when he was on earth*. The Lord Jesus never spoke one word which suggested that any of the Ten Commandments would ever be abolished. On the contrary, he declared, "I did not come to destroy but to fulfil" (Matthew 5:17), and I am satisfied that he spoke these words with reference to the moral law of the Ten Commandments. The Lord Jesus spoke of the Ten Commandments as a recognised standard of moral right and wrong (Mark 10:19). When he spoke about the Sabbath it was always to correct the superstitious *additions* which the Pharisees had added to the Law of Moses. He said nothing to suggest that the great principle itself would ever be changed.

e. Turn now to *the writings of the apostles*. The apostles speak much about the temporary nature of the ceremonial law. But they never suggest that any of the Ten Commandments is abolished. On the contrary, they appeal to them as an accepted standard of Christian conduct. For example, when Paul wants to teach the duty of children to parents, he simply quotes the Fifth Commandment, "Honour your father and mother, which is the first commandment with promise" (Ephesians 6:1).

f. Turn now to *the practice of the apostles*. There is great emphasis in the New Testament upon the "first day of the week" (See Matthew 28:1, Mark 16:2,9, Luke 24:1, John

138

20:1,19, Acts 20:7, 1 Corinthians 16:2.) It is clear that the apostles kept this day - the day of the Lord's resurrection - as a holy day. We see in Acts 20:7 that this was the day on which the disciples "came together to break bread". We see in 1 Corinthians 16:2 that this was the day on which they were to contribute to the "collection for the saints". Revelation 1:10 speaks of this day as "the Lord's Day".

Now it is obvious that this "Lord's Day" was not the same day of the week as the Jewish sabbath. Under the inspiration of God, the apostles changed from the seventh day to the first day, because that was the day on which the Lord Jesus was raised from the dead. But the *principle* remains the same. It is one day in seven set apart for God. The spirit of the Fourth Commandment is not changed in the least. The Lord's Day, on the first day of the week, is just as much a day of rest after six days' labour as the seventh-day sabbath had been.

I ask you, then, to pay very serious attention to these arguments from Scripture. It seems clear to me that God's people in every generation have kept one day in seven as God's day, and that we must do the same.

2. The purpose of the Lord's Day

Why has God appointed that one day in seven should be set apart for himself? We must be clear about this, for it is not difficult to understand. *He has given it to us for our good.* The day was never set apart to be a burden, but a blessing. It is in God's mercy that he has given us this Day. It is for the good of all mankind.

First, *it is good for man's body*. We all need a day of rest. Our bodies cannot function properly without regular periods of rest, and God has provided this for us.

Secondly, *it is good for man's mind*. The mind needs regular rest just as much as the body does.

Thirdly, *it is good for society*. The society which recognises God's day will benefit in two ways. It is good for the character

139

of its people, and it tends to produce prosperity. People who regularly rest one day in seven will do more, and better, work in a year than people who do not have this pattern of work and rest. Their bodies will be stronger and their minds clearer. Their power to apply themselves to their work and to persevere with it will be greater.

Fourthly, *it is an unmixed good for man's soul*. The soul has needs just as much as the mind and body. In this world, we are tempted to become caught up in our earthly concerns and to forget about our spiritual well-being. The appointment of one day in seven as a day set apart for God is a most wise and merciful provision to prevent this. The Lord's Day becomes a kind of foretaste of heaven, reminding us that one day we shall be taken away from this world altogether. But where the day is neglected, it is generally the case that a man's Christian faith deteriorates badly.

We should understand, then, that to have one day set apart for God is a great privilege. It is altogether for our good, and it is a privilege which we should highly prize.

3. How the Lord's Day should be kept

In seeking to know how we should keep the Lord's Day, our concern must not be with the differing opinions of men, but with the will of God revealed in his Word. There we find two general rules laid down for our guidance. All specific questions must be decided by these two general rules.

The first plain rule is that the Lord's Day must be kept as *a day of rest*. Of course, works of necessity and of mercy may be done, as the Lord Jesus himself plainly teaches. It is right to do whatever is necessary to preserve and maintain life - whether human life, or the life of our animals - and to do good to the souls of men. But as far as possible, all work ought to cease - both mental work and physical work. This is made plain in the fourth commandment: "You shall do no work: you, nor your son, nor your daughter, nor your manservant, nor your maidservant, nor your cattle, nor your stranger who is within your gates" (Exodus 20:10).

The second great rule is that the Lord's Day must be kept *holy*. The "rest" of the Lord's Day is to be a *holy* rest. It is to be a rest in which we attend to the affairs of our souls, to eternal matters, and to communion with God and Christ. It is *the Lord's* Day.

Large numbers of people make no attempt to keep the day holy. Many spend the day in social activities, business dealings, travelling, reading newspapers or novels, talking about politics, or in idle gossip. For them it is a day for anything rather than the things of God. This kind of thing is completely wrong. I know that many act in ignorance, simply doing what their fathers have done before them, but it does not alter the fact that it is utterly wrong. It is impossible to say that those who spend the day in such ways are keeping it "holy". However small these matters may seem to be, they are things which prevent men from seeking God on his Day, and getting benefit from it.

Those who create work for others on God's Day are equally wrong. *Everyone* needs the day of rest and worship which God has appointed. It is not only for you, but also for "your son, your daughter, your manservant, your maidservant, your ox, your donkey, your cattle, your stranger who is within your gates, *that your manservant and your maidservant may rest as well as you*" (Deuteronomy 5:14).

I am not a Pharisee. I do not for a moment want a hard-working man who has been shut up indoors for six working days to suppose that I object to his taking lawful relaxation for his body on the Lord's Day. I see no harm in a quiet walk on a Sunday, provided that it does not take the place of going to public worship, and that it genuinely is quiet, like that of Isaac in Genesis 24:63. Our Lord and his disciples walked through the cornfields on the Sabbath. But I do say, Beware that you do not turn this liberty into license. Beware that you do not injure the spiritual well-being of others while seeking relaxation for yourself. Remember that you have a soul as well as a body to attend to.

I am not advocating fanaticism. I do not tell anyone that he ought to pray all day, or read his Bible all day, or go to church all day, or meditate all day on Sunday. All I ask is that Sunday be kept as a *holy rest*. God should be kept in view. His Word should be studied. We should meet for worship with his people. The great matters of our spiritual well-being should be attended to. I say, therefore, that anything which prevents the day being kept holy in this way ought, as far as possible, to be avoided.

I do not admire any kind of gloomy religion. Please do not think I want the Lord's Day to be a day of sadness and unhappiness. I want every Christian to be a happy man. I want him to have "joy and peace in believing" and to "rejoice in hope of the glory of God". I want everyone to regard the Lord's Day as the brightest, most cheerful day of the week. If you think that the kind of Sunday which I am advocating would be a wearisome day, then I must tell you that there is something wrong with the state of your heart. If you cannot *enjoy* a holy Sunday, the fault is not in the day but in your own heart.

Many will think that I am setting far too high a standard of keeping the Lord's Day. Those who do not like to think about spiritual things, those who are worldly, lovers of money and lovers of pleasure will say that what I am asking is impossible. But the only question with which I am concerned is this - What does the Bible teach? We must not bring God's standards down to man's, but rather take our standards from the Word of God.

What I am teaching about keeping the Lord's Day is only what all the best and holiest Christians of every church and nation have taught and practised. There have hardly been any exceptions. It is extraordinary to observe the agreement among them on this point. Those who have disagreed widely on many points - even about the grounds on which we should keep the Lord's Day - have shown a remarkable degree of unity about how it should be kept.

142

I believe that anyone who calmly and rationally thinks about things to come will realise that the standard of keeping the Lord's Day which I am advocating is not too high. Is it true that we all must die? - that we must all appear before God? If so, surely it is not too much to give one day in seven to God. It is not too much to test our own fitness for the presence of God by spending his Day in special preparation for it. I believe that common sense, reason and conscience will all combine to tell us that if we cannot spare one day a week for God in this life, we are not living as those who hope to spend eternity with him.

A final appeal

1. I appeal to all who do not keep the Lord's Day holy. I want to remind you that you must give an account to God on the great Day of Judgment. But how unfit you are to appear before God! You are not prepared for the presence of God. On earth, you cannot give God one day out of every seven. It wearies you to spend just a seventh of your time in getting to know him. How then could you possibly be fit to spend eternity with him?

I appeal to you: Stop and think! Repent, and change your ways! Confess your sin at the Throne of Grace, and ask pardon through that blood which "cleanses from all sin". Begin immediately to attend a church where you will hear the gospel preached. Arrange your time on Sunday so that you can quietly and seriously meditate on eternal things. Avoid all company which would lead you to talk only about this world. Take out your Bible, and begin to read it seriously. I appeal to you to do these things, and to do them without delay. It may be hard at first, but it is well worth the struggle. Do it, for the eternal well-being of your soul!

2. I appeal lastly to all who sincerely love the Lord Jesus Christ and desire to serve him. First, I ask you to examine your own practice in keeping the Lord's Day holy. Are you using the day as carefully as you ought? Secondly, I ask you to do all you

can to promote the keeping of God's Day by others. But remember that it is not enough to be negative, and to protest about the way people treat God's Day. We must evangelise. We must preach the good news of Christ. We must show people a better way. Only then will we see societies transformed, and men and women truly seeking and honouring God on the Lord's Day.